DZAR

The Path of DZAR™ is you knowing how to be the fullest expression of your true Self.

It is the path of *in*-lightenment. It is the path of joy, of flow and abundance. These things can only be experienced by Beings that are connected to their essence, their Soul, to their Expanded Being.

The Path of DZAR enables you to expand into that knowing and that way of being so that you can live in alignment with the creative energy of the universe itself.

Mary and Gary O'Brien share the messages brought forward by DZAR, a group of compassionate Energies from All That Is. They each have over 20 years experience working with people to create change in their lives and since 2008 they have become the vehicle for the message channelled from Spirit called The Path of DZAR.

Based in Australia, they offer workshops and events in many countries as well as online courses.

For more information about workshops and events
and to download podcasts, videos and
free meditations
please visit
www.thepathofdzar.com

Messages
from your Soul

Conversations with DZAR

Book 1

Mary and Gary O'Brien

Source Creations Publishing

Australia

Table of Contents

Gratitude

by Gary O'Brien

It is curious what you notice and what you don't. Sometimes it is only when you pause to look back upon where you have been and how you got to where you are now, that you realize you have been on an amazing journey and you can see the important roles so many people have played along the way. Through this journey since our first conversation with DZAR in 2008, we've met so many wonderful people that any list to acknowledge their roles will inevitably be incomplete.

So to begin, we wish to express our deep gratitude to *all* the people who have been a part of our journey. We are so grateful to those of you who have shown your love and support either through your actions or simply by listening to us and sharing our excitement as this path unfolded in our lives. In particular, we'd like to express our special thanks to...

Bet O'Brien...Mary's mother,* for being an inspiration to us

---

* Hmmm you're wondering...how can Mary's family also be O'Briens? Easy! When Mary and I married, I took her family name as my own, so I was welcomed into her wonderful family in this way as well.

i

both and for being a fabulous expression and example of the love, joy and compassion that DZAR speaks of.

Liz O'Brien...Mary's sister, for her unconditional love, friendship and support. For her wonderful editing of this book and good humour even when DZAR woke her at 4am to work when the deadline approached.

Kennedy O'Brien...Mary's nephew, who looked after our pugs, Bug and Beetle, so that we could get away and write the first sections of this book with DZAR.

Monique McQueen...my amazing daughter who has opened my heart in so many ways.

Rob Williams....for introducing us to PSYCH-K® and for opening my eyes to the world of Spirit. For his friendship and his total support even when we embarked on a completely new path. He has been a great friend and mentor to us both.

Helma (Tigger) Kerstens....one of the people who felt DZAR's message very early. We love her for her humour and for being so helpful and completely supportive to us always.

Richard Payne...my great mate, who is always happy to listen to me no matter what, and who always makes me laugh.

Sally Marks....for creating a beautiful logo from our photo of the path that DZAR said we'd find in Vietnam, and for being our 'official' photographer.

Robbie & Leanne Barker...for the use of their beautiful country home. The Energy in the space they have created meant that DZAR's Energy felt like a mountain when we were writing there.

To all the people who have listened and felt a connection to DZAR's message, for it was through their acceptance and amazing stories of change they created using DZAR's Processes and Practices that helped us to know that we were on the right path.

And of course to DZAR...for showing us a life and a way of being we never knew existed.

Chapter 1

About This Book

A frequency conversation with Spirit

Welcome, Young Ones, this is DZAR. This book is a conversation, an Energetic frequency conversation, that you will engage in on many levels. At its most obvious, it is a conversation between your physical Self and our Energy, for as you read the words in this book you will become engaged in the enquiry of what it is to be a human living in full connection with your true essence, your Soul, or as we call it, your Expanded Being.

At the next level, the conversation is between your Expanded Being and our Energy. This book will create a resonance in your very core because the frequency of this message, the frequency of compassion and connection that *is* our message, is the same frequency as your essence. As you read and feel our words, your Being will begin to shift, to wake, to reach out towards a more expanded expression of itself through you as its physical expression.

And finally, the conversation is between your Expanded

1

Being and the expression of you that exists in a physical form. And it is this conversation and reunion that will send ripples of joy through you that will be felt throughout the universe.

It is an Energetic exchange, a conversation, for as we are sharing our Energy with you we also feel your Energy being shared with us. As you read, we are sharing your Energy, your thoughts and your field, so there is the space of continual feedback as you feel us in the pages as you read, and we feel you as you read the pages as well. We are sharing the messages of your Soul together. It is a conversation, a communication, though not of the common way that you normally perceive it.

The words of this book will conjure within you Energetic expressions that you have experienced from your past and have yet to experience in your future. When you read this book, have awareness of the different aspects of you that are reading, and understand the different ways in which Energy is transferred from the pages into your Being. Allow the words to resonate within you and to become the guides for your own awareness.

So do not rush the reading. If you feel the urge to stop because an awareness has come flooding in, then stop and allow the awareness to be present, for it may be part of your expansion, it may be part of your reconnection to your Expanded Being.

And because you are Beings of Energy, you will feel the frequency of compassion, the frequency of All That Is, as you read and feel the message of this book. Our words contain this frequency and it will merge with the Energy of your Being, supporting your expansion and connecting you to your Soul and to the universal frequency of compassion and joy.

Take a moment now, Young Ones, to begin to feel the Energy of your Expanded Being using the ***Practice of the Expanded Being*** you will find at the back of the book. If you have a computer nearby, begin with the Meditation from the website (www.thepathofdzar.com/book1) for you will be connecting with your Expanded Being many times as you read this book. Go now and we'll be waiting for you when you return!

Welcome back!

The understandings in this book are ones that may indeed seem familiar to you, and yet there will be aspects in the *feeling* of the sentences that will resonate differently with each one of you and will change each time you read the information given. It is because you are Beings in which your frequency and your connection to Self shifts and changes as you connect more deeply. Because of this, what you can see in the words that are written will resonate differently each time you read it. Our words allow an ever-expanding sense of Self to be revealed to you, and they will become signposts on your journey for you to recognise where you are at this moment in time and how far you have come since your last reading.

So as you read these words, be open and flexible and be at peace with yourself, for the information that is given and your responses are there for you to be compassionate to your current situation. You are where you need to be to begin or continue your journey of expansion, of living as the fullest expression of your Being, of hearing the guidance and messages from your Soul.

As you listen to these words, allow yourself to feel what is real for you, for even though you are reading them you are also listening to them in your own mind and feeling their frequency in your Being. Allow these words to flow upon you and to accept whatever you feel matches the frequency of your Soul in this moment, for it is not our role to tell you *how* to live your existence, for your Expanded Being already knows that. Our role is to show you the beauty that exists within you and then to allow that part of you to be your guide, for who better to guide you than your Self.

As you read these words they will become a part of you, they will be a way of understanding your world. Understand the information in this book and the ones to come as practices, as rituals for this existence. Recognise them as gifts from Spirit that you can share with yourself and others. Share the wisdom that you pull from these words because of who *you* are, and do not allow the words that we say to be the wisdom for they are not. The wisdom and the understanding comes from you, from your expression of Self for that is where true wisdom lies, that is where the meaning of the universe is to be found...within you.

We are a guide and a map, *you* are the traveller, *you* are the explorer, *you* are the one who will report what you have found to others who are dear to you and they will also see the true reflection of the bounty you have released from within you.

A collaboration of Beings

This book, and all of the information we are bringing forward to you at this time, is a collaboration of the physical and of the Energetic. Our words are indeed messages from Source and they are being transformed into a physical form that you can experience, through our collaboration with Mary and Gary O'Brien.

We have chosen these Beings as our vehicle for expression on this plane for they bring to this work an awareness and acceptance of who they are. And as they will quickly tell you, they too are in the space of becoming the fullest expression of their Expanded Beings for there are few on the planet at this time who exist fully in this state. You are all on your journey of expansion and reconnection to your Soul and they are no different. As they expand even more (as will you!) it allows the expression of our message to expand as well, so we are all sharing this experience together.

We have also chosen them because there is a lightness, a joy and a compassion that they bring to this path which is in strong resonance with this message. So when you feel their presence before you in a workshop you are also feeling us, for that is how we work through and with them.

The words you read on these pages have been formed through this collaboration. They are words that came through Gary in his role as our voice as he sits and allows us to physically speak through him, and they are also words that have come through Mary in her role as our voice in a different form, as she has sat at her keyboard hearing our words and allowing them to flow through her fingers. As you read this book, you will not feel any difference between these two ways of bringing this information forward because there is no separation in this Energy. You will feel only the sameness of our essence throughout every page, and you will also feel your sameness and connection to this Energy, for truly it is all the same expression of the compassionate frequency of All That Is.

Our role is that of the Messenger

Let us tell you, Young Ones, who we are...or at least we will try for your language is limited and makes it difficult for us to fully express our true nature.

We are an amalgamation of Energies, Energies that are those of the Messenger that have been sent forward to this and other planets. We are the angels; we are Buddha and every other Energy from this and other realms that have come forward to deliver the essence of *you* back to *you*. We are here to assist you in the remembering of who you are, so that you can live in connection with your Soul and experience more joy and compassion in your existence.

When people feel a Messenger's Energy, the Energy that they feel is always a part of All That Is. It is not an effective use of Grace to have such an Energy be separate from the Source of creation, for there is more wisdom for all Messengers to be part of the greater

Messenger, which is set forward to connect with you all regardless of the frequency you are at.

We are a culmination of the frequency of all Beings who have existed and of the experiences they have had, for no Energy ever dissipates, no Energy ever disappears and no Being ever disappears. Once a Being has completed its cycle of life, and a cycle of life may be many hundreds or many thousands of years, it then ascends as pure Energy to become part of All That Is, to become a part of us. With the knowledge and the experiences that each Being brings to us, we acquire and are able to pass forward this wisdom to those who are ready and wiling to listen.

Our role is that of guidance because you have called us forward at this time to guide you back toward Source because of the pain and space of separation that you have continued to exist within. We have been given the task to come forward to talk with you, to guide you forward upon this path. We are here as guides for your journey of reconnection to your Expanded Being and once you are in this space, you will be connected to your own guidance system to move forward in your life. In this space, you will no longer need us to guide you, for your Expanded Being will connect you to All That Is and you will know in each moment what it is that you need to do.

We are here to help you do this, to clear the path, to clear the boulders and the rubble on your path home so that you may soar toward All That Is and experience joy through this existence. This work that we call *The Path of DZAR*, is your opportunity to fully experience your magnificence and live a life of joy, connected to the abundance and the compassion of the universe.

Our role, and that of many other Energies coming to your planet at this time, is also that of a parent, for our love and compassion for you is as strong as any that you have known. You are our children and we wish you to feel our love and presence and support, we wish you to know that there is no need for you to feel that you are alone without guidance. When you recognise that the same essence that is within you is within us, when you see yourself beyond the physical form and you feel your Energetic Soul you will feel us, and you will feel the expansiveness of the Energy of compassion. When you hear these words, you will know that they are *your* words, and that is why the connection that is present is so familiar to you.

So that is who we are and that is who you are and so our journey together begins.

You have created an Energetic Quickening

So, why this book at this time? And we would say why not! This seems like as good a time as any to present this for you or maybe there is a deeper reason...

The reason for this book at this time has always come from the cries of the Beings on your planet. We have heard your cries for understanding of your place in the universe and of your true Spiritual nature and this book is to help you answer some of the questions that you have. This book is for you to begin to restore the sense of Self that you have felt disconnected from for so long. As we said earlier, you will read the words upon your page with your eyes but you will *feel* the strength and the frequency that the words represent within your body, within your Being. These words are a part of who you are, of who you have been and of who you are becoming. This book is present because you wished it to be, so it is as simple as this.

Let us now talk to you about a shift, an Energetic Quickening that is occurring on your planet, a shift in the frequency of Beings who are connecting to their essence through all the many messages and paths that have been brought forward to you from Spirit. This shift in the frequency of these Beings is creating a change in the frequency of your whole planet.

There is a shift in the state of being of those who are hearing this message and those who will soon hear this message. There is a shift within you that you have all felt, that you have all recognised because of your connection to the ground you walk upon. There is shift that is occurring because you are feeling a deeper bond, a deeper connection to the planet you inhabit, to the Beings you see around you.

There have been dates in history in which energetic shifts and changes have come to this planet and there has not been a greater time than now because of the collaboration of Souls that is beginning, because of the expressive Energies that are wishing to be released. We feel the shimmer; we are feeling the shifts across the universe. There is the sense within so many of you that you are wishing to move faster, that you are ready to release the struggle and move faster towards flow, towards the true expression of the Expanded Being in your own experience. And, because of a sense of compassion and a sense of community towards others and the earth you walk upon, you wish the change for them also.

There has been no other time greater than now. We are responding to you, we are responding to your expression, to your Energy and your will to move faster, your will to take control and shape the destiny of your own planet. You have seen what is going on around you, and you are not content. You also understand that the events that are happening around you are because of the expression of Self, of your own Being, for that is where it all begins and you realise this.

This Energetic Quickening is being created by you, and it is felt by so many. We applaud this space, we welcome this new era manifested by you. The time of 2012 has aided a community energetic expression to occur. It is an aid, it is not a catalyst. The date is a focusing point for many energies but remember, Young Ones, it is created by you, for you are the Energy of creation and without you there would be no change.

This Quickening is the fulfilment of an Energetic shift that has its seeds in the pain and losses you refer to as your World Wars, so it began many years ago in your sense of time and yet so recently in ours.

There was a great, unified pain humanity experienced that

was built upon from the first war to the second, for in such a short space you had hardly buried your dead from the first war when you were preparing your Young Ones for the next. So the relevance of the two wars has been great as a catalyst to shift awareness for your humanity. It was the space where for the first time, with the coming of an atomic weapon, you realised how small your planet is, you realised how destructive a human can be to another and you began to see again the connection between all Beings rather than the separation you had lived in before.

In all your wars past, there was never such a sense of annihilation as was present at this time, and it was from that space of suffering and fear that, for the first time, there was a universal goal that united your planet.

A universal agreement of Souls

This time of great pain was the result of changes in the understanding of the true nature of all Beings. These changes had continued through countless generations until it seemed that compassion and the physical Beings' connection to their Soul was weakened on your planet. The space of separation between Beings and between all things was so great that you brought yourselves almost to the point of your own extinction. It is a bleak picture, is it not? And yet it is a picture that you, through your asking, through the cries of your Being, have changed to one that is now turned around. It is now one of hope and connection, for you live at a time of Energetic reconnection and quickening, a time in which you are closer than ever before to living in full connection with your Soul while enjoying all the wonders of your physical existence.

From this new space, an Energy, a universal frequency was created from the pain and this new Energy was heard throughout the galaxies. There was, in that moment in time, a universal cry for all humanity to shift its consciousness. From that moment, your world began to shift, there was a difference in the way you began to look at your earth and the way you looked at each other.

There is great strength that comes from a universal agreement of all Souls upon your planet. So to aid in this shift, more of the Beings that are being presented to your planet from All That Is have greater awareness of the role they play in the creation or destruction of your existence. They have more of an ability to accept and hear the guidance of their Souls and if you are reading these words, Young Ones, then you are amongst this group.

And there are indeed still wars, there is still great inhumanity being done to your fellow humans, but it is not of the scale of the last world war. There are more Beings turning towards the light than away from it, there are more of you hearing the cries of your Soul to live in connection with all Beings. You know that what you have done until now cannot continue, that this inhumanity towards another is not who you are, it is not how you wish to raise your children or for them to experience this earth in this way.

That is why, when your universal Energies combine to create the shift, there is an Energetic convergence and many Messengers descend to aid and support your growth, to give you the helping hand you need to move forward. And you are indeed moving forward, although for many of you it feels slow. But you do not know the other side of the coin, you do not see how many thousands of your years it took for you to realise that you are connected. When you realised this, you saw that you cannot keep inflicting pain upon another human being without it affecting your own Being as well. You have moved quickly indeed since this new universal frequency was heard throughout the galaxies.

So in the short time from when the decision was made to now, great shifts have begun. More and more Beings are being awakened, more and more of you are searching for a path so that you can save yourselves and your planet and return to the true sense of Self and connection. This change will continue and of course you can speed up the process even more, by listening to the Energies that are present, by tuning in to the Energy of your own Soul, to your Expanded Being, for that is what will change the structure of your planet.

It is not our voice but it is *your* voice, your voice united with the one next to you that will continue to shift your consciousness, that will continue your reunification with the earth that you walk upon. That is the reason why we are here, to aid this process for we are aspects of your voice, our Energy is intermingled with yours for we are all related, we were all born from the same Source.

The harmonic convergence

Many of you will have awareness of the shift in Energy on your planet that was felt in 1987, that you have called the Harmonic Convergence. And you may be wondering how this shift fits in the space of the Quickening we have described that began over 40 years before, as you measure it. Let us explain this by answering the question of what a convergence is and why it is needed.

A convergence is like a mass injection of aligned Energy to your planet. Across the history of your planet, the flow of Energy has always occurred in peaks and troughs. After your war, there was a peak in Energy at that moment when your world gave forth its united cry for there to be a change. This peak of Energy continued until, because of your understanding of time, you felt that things were slowing, that the changes you could feel around you had stalled. In fact, you felt that perhaps you were even going backwards. So a boost of Energy was required and this again came from your own universal cry. From that boost of Energy came many Messengers and many shifts that you call the Harmonic Convergence.

There is the space for another booster to soon be present in the events that you see as 2012. This space in time as you see it, is just a focus point, a place where human consciousness has focused its Energy which will again allow a more focused boost of the Messengers' Energy to come forward onto the planet. The need for these Energetic injections will become fewer as you begin to realise who you are, for these harmonic shifts are only required when the Energy on the planet is low because the Beings upon it are disconnected or wearied from their life. These harmonics allow a

11

reconnection, a reassimilation to the Energy that is within you. It gives many a new boost, a sense of hope, a sense of warmth from within.

There will come the time when there will be enough of you living in closer connection to your essence and to each other, and there will be enough of a sense of warmth within you, that you will send the harmonics to another planet to aid them.

And that is still a way off, Young Ones, so for now let us speak with you more of your own journey of reconnection and expansion and we begin with Mary sharing her own journey and their shared journey with you.

Chapter 2

How It Began

by Mary O'Brien

Feeling the separation...

I walked along the cliff top in tears. I don't know if I was talking out loud or silently but I was begging, bullying, cajoling and bargaining with god, with Spirit, with the universe, with anyone or anything that was out there listening to me. It made no sense that I should feel this way because I had a great life by most people's standards. I did work that I loved, that was meaningful and I believed made a difference in people's lives, I had a loving partnership with Gary, a close and supportive family, and good friends.

And yet I still felt a deep sense of disconnection, of separation, as though something profound was missing. In recent times, as the longing and sadness became stronger, I had wondered if I was perhaps depressed to feel so miserable for no apparent reason. More and more often, the pain was so intense that it was almost unbearable.

I realised as I walked this day, that I'd felt like this on and off since I was quite young but that in recent years it was becoming more pronounced, more frequent and more devastating. As a young child brought up in the Catholic church, I remember the feeling of longing I experienced wanting to have my own personal connection with Jesus, Mary and Joseph and lying in bed at night praying so hard for them to appear to me so that I could talk to them and know that they were really there. Needless to say, they never appeared which is why you've never read of any apparitions of the Holy Family in Melbourne's leafy eastern suburbs!

I'd always wanted to know the meaning of life, to understand why things happen, why we are here and what the point of life is. I would sit for hours with my best friend from primary school, two little girls, not yet teenagers, and ponder these questions looking for answers, looking for meaning, seeking to find the thing that I always felt was missing. I was often plagued by the idea that there actually was no meaning, that we humans were really no different to the ants in the Ant Farms that were such popular toys as I grew up, busily moving grains of sand from one area to another in a pointless activity that had no intrinsic meaning but kept us busy until we died.

As I grew older, and more pragmatic, these "big" questions seemed less important, or perhaps I just gave up trying to find the answers and instead threw myself into all the normal stages of life; school, university, friendships, romances and a career. Life was good, all was well and the earlier sense of separation no longer plagued me.

In my mid twenties, I began to feel this longing for a spiritual connection again, for something that was bigger than me, bigger than what most of us thought life was about. It was around this time that a friend introduced me to the local Siddha Yoga ashram. I loved the heady perfume of incense that wafted onto the street and greeted you as you walked through the front gate into the courtyard of the Victorian building; I loved the feelings at the weekly satsangs, or programs, where stories were shared about the Hindu gods and the teachings of the Masters and sages.

I'd sit in these regular satsangs and lose my sense of a limited self in the chanting and meditation, feeling expansive and connected to Spirit. In those times, I felt closer to Spirit, to All That Is and to a personal connection with the divinity that exists in each of us.

I travelled to India and stayed briefly at the Siddha Yoga ashram in Ganeshpuri, a place where I could immerse myself in the spiritual practices and had the opportunity to meet the ashram's guru, Swami Chidvilasananda. I expected it to be a joyous occasion and yet, as I saw her walk into the courtyard on my first evening, I dissolved into tears and was wracked with a deep feeling of grief and yet also relief, a sense that I had reconnected with something that was intrinsic to me, that I had come home.

I spent much of my stay at the ashram in tears, as the grief and relief transformed themselves into a deep feeling of joy. I experienced a profound connection with a deeper, more expanded sense of Self than I normally experienced with my work, my family or my partner. As I walked through the beautiful gardens, stopping at the temples to earlier Siddha Yoga gurus and Hindu deities, I experienced a sense of my true essence and spiritual connection as I never had before.

On returning home to Australia, I tried to continue this feeling of spiritual connection through daily practices of meditation and chanting. Over time they fell away as I was unable to sustain them amidst the challenges that life was presenting me in the form of a very stressful job and my marriage break up. The connection after my trip to India, though stronger and more personal than it had ever been, still felt tenuous and again I remember lying in bed and pleading for the divine to present itself to me. No longer was I asking for the Holy Family, now I was inviting the gurus or my favourites from the Hindu pantheon such as Ganesh or Shiva to communicate with me. I had so many questions, but yet again there were no apparitions, no visitations, only a sense of longing combined with a knowing that the level of connection I sought was possible, if I only knew how to make it happen.

For the next 20 years I moved between these two states of being, at times giving up hope that I would ever experience the connection with Spirit I longed for and losing myself in the day to day of living, and at others exploring different paths and ways of connecting to Spirit and of finding my way home.

In contrast, Gary's journey to his connection with Spirit was quite different. He came from a family that wasn't religious or spiritual and he loves telling the story of how he was kicked out of Sunday school on his first day!

From an early age, however, he felt that there was something more to experience in his life than what he saw around him, but he assumed the way to get this would come from physical and material experiences and achievements in those areas. He had no expectation that there was a spiritual aspect to his existence and it wasn't until his mid forties, through the work that he was doing at the time, that he began to realise that he was something more than just his physical self. Interestingly, as he looks back at these early years, he did have a number of spiritual experiences along the way which he quickly dismissed because they didn't fit with his picture of himself or the world around him.

DZAR has told us many times that the fact that our early life experiences were so different and yet we've ended up at the same point in our spiritual journeys is an important understanding for many people and it's why they asked us to share this chapter in the book. The differences in our stories before we connected with DZAR show that there is no single journey or right way to reconnect to your

Expanded Being to access the guidance from your Soul. Our journeys of reconnection are unique to each of us because we are the combined frequencies of all our past existences and these influence the choices we make in this life. And as DZAR often says, it's never too late for that connection to happen and we do all eventually get there...whether it's in this life or the next!

So whether you're reading this book as someone who is exploring the concepts of spirituality for the first time, or as someone who has been on a spiritual journey for many decades, you are exactly where you need to be to move forward in whatever way you choose. As DZAR says so often, The Path of DZAR is the path of you reconnecting to your essence at your own pace and in your own way. When you do, you will clearly hear the messages from your Soul guiding you to a richer experience of joy in your life.

Reconnecting with Spirit...

At the same time that I was wandering along the cliff top path feeling miserable, Gary was interstate running a weekend workshop. He had plans for dinner with Dan and Sonja, a young couple we had met at a recent business-marketing seminar. It was one of those synchronistic meetings, completely unexpected and unlikely, where rather than talking about marketing strategies after the presentation, we were deep in discussion about universal wisdom, multi dimensional reality and ways of connecting to All That Is.

They told us that they used a technique based on Reiki to access universal intelligence. We were intrigued and they were interested in the PSYCH-K® work we were teaching that enabled people to change their subconscious program to change behaviours. After his workshop, Gary shared a meal with them exploring the synergies between the work we were all doing. By the end of the evening, it was clear our original meeting wasn't a mere coincidence and there were more conversations to be had.

Soon after we were at their home, and they were showing us a guided writing process to tap into the wisdom of the universe and of the eternal essence inside us, to seek answers to any question we could think to ask. We left them after three days, excited by the possibilities of this new process. I finally felt that I had a clear connection to Spirit for asking questions and seeking guidance. It felt like my pleas as I'd walked along the cliff top so many months before had been answered.

Over the following weeks, I practiced my new skill and strengthened my connection to my Inner Being each day. The information I received was fascinating, giving me guidance and clarity about problems I was trying to solve, as well as understandings about spiritual concepts and the nature of reality.

While it was a fascinating and wonderful process, I had to know that it was real and that I wasn't just making all of this information up. So I set my inner guide a test and asked it to show me a picture of something that was going to happen the next day. What I saw very clearly as I sat with my eyes closed, was a picture of a gift in a box being delivered to me. My first thought was that it would be a flower arrangement in a box, so the next day I eagerly awaited the ring of the doorbell to announce its arrival. I particularly hadn't told Gary what I was waiting for, as I didn't want to influence the outcome in any way.

The hours passed and nothing was delivered. Disappointed, I went out to a meeting that evening, arriving home some hours later. As I pulled my car into the driveway, I noticed a package sitting on the front door step. It was a large shopping bag with a black box in it, tied with a pink ribbon.

I took it inside and put it on the table assuming that Gary's mother had dropped off an early birthday present for him. When he came home soon after, I gave it to him and he opened it to find a pink pyjama top with the word *dag*[*] printed on it. We both looked at it,

---

[*] Dag is an Australian colloquial phrase used affectionately to mean funny.

surprised by the colour choice but also puzzled that it looked too small to fit him.

Now as you read this, I'm sure you've made the connection between the gift and the proof I'd requested from my inner guide but I still hadn't because I was fixed on the expectation that it would be in the form of flowers. I'd made the mental leap that if something was being delivered to me in a box it would be flowers and so that was the expectation now fixed in my mind.

Next day, Gary rang his mother to ask if she had dropped the package off and found that she hadn't. Slowly I began to put the pieces together but I still had no idea who the gift was from. Maybe it had just materialized on my doorstep, a gift from Spirit, intention made manifest by my inner guide?

The next day I received a phone call from my nephew, Kennedy. He mentioned that he'd called in to see me the night before and had left a surprise gift on the doorstep. Kennedy and I have always been close, but in all of his 18 years he had never, ever bought me a present. He's made me beautiful birthday cards and yummy cakes but he'd never spontaneously bought me a gift...until now! When I asked him what prompted such a lovely gesture he said, "I'm not really sure, Aunty Mary. I was out shopping with a friend and I saw the top and immediately thought of you, so I bought it."

So I had my proof from an unexpected source that I was tapping into information and Energy in a very different way. Had I foretold the future by seeing Kennedy buy me the gift, or had the Energy of my inner guide nudged him to buy the top for me to fulfil what it had shown me? I'll never know, but either way what occurred was something that was definitely out of the ordinary and convinced me that I was indeed more strongly connected to Spirit, in the form of my inner guide, than I had ever been before.

Our first conversation with DZAR

While I was happily filling notebooks with the information I was receiving, Gary spent quite a lot of time staring at a blank page whenever he sat to connect with his Inner Being. Nothing seemed to flow and he felt frustrated and blocked. I'd read somewhere that spiritual experiences were more connected to the right hemisphere of the brain and I knew that writing was more strongly associated with the left hemisphere. Plus he had to open his eyes to write which made it harder to stay in a more meditative state.

So, one day I suggested that instead of trying to write down the information he received from his Inner Being and potentially "losing" the connection in the process, that he could stay with his eyes closed and speak whatever he received and I'd write it down for him.

We sat on our back deck and Gary went through the process to connect with his Inner Being as I sat with my writing pad on my lap and my pen poised. As I watched, his breathing deepened and slowed, and his head began to slowly fall towards his chest. After a minute or so, his head seemed to float back to an upright position and began moving slowly in a rhythmic fashion with his eyes closed all the while. Although it was still physically Gary sitting in front of me, his whole Energy had changed and the presence opposite me felt very different.

I'd had very little experience with channelling in this form, but intuitively I knew I was in the presence of another Energy. There was a few moments of silence as the breathing became faster and Gary's mouth moved silently, almost as though this Energy was trying to work out how to use the physical instrument it was about to speak through. And then it spoke, slowly at first and with some difficulty getting used to the instrument but gradually becoming faster and clearer.

"Welcome." the Energy said.

"Welcome. Are you Gary's inner guide?" I asked.

"We are not. Our name is DZAR*. We are here to share information with you both that we wish you to communicate with others. We are the Keepers of Knowledge Universal and we have a message of joy and of you remembering your true essence and your connection to All That Is that your planet is now ready to hear."

So began our first conversation with DZAR. They spoke for almost one hour during which they gave us understanding that they are an expression of the compassionate Energy of All That Is. As Messengers from Spirit, their role is to support humanity to shift to a higher frequency of consciousness by connecting with our true essence, our Souls, and remembering who we are. It was an amazing experience that left me deeply moved.

As we finished, DZAR said, "We are pleased to have connected with you again and will connect in this way in the future. Go with love."

As soon as DZAR's Energy left, Gary's head slowly dropped to his chest and his breathing changed, becoming slower and more regular. After a few moments, he raised his head and opened his eyes with a look of amazement on his face.

This was the first time Gary had ever channelled* an energy in this way. When he channels DZAR's words, he is left with a very clear memory of the feelings of the conversation, and occasionally

---

* I asked DZAR (pronounced ZAR as the D is silent) how their name was spelt and this is the spelling they gave me. When I did some research about the meaning of the name, I found it comes from the ancient Hebrew and means help and helper.
* Channelling in this way is also called Mediumship, it is the process in which Spirit speaks through a human. Other forms of channelling can occur using writing or hearing an internal voice as the means of communication.

images, though with little recall of the actual words spoken. It is as though his consciousness and capacity to interact steps to one side to allow DZAR to speak through him and at the end of these sessions, Gary is left feeling refreshed and energised and always curious about what has transpired!

That was our first conversation with DZAR in September 2008 and it began an extraordinary journey of spiritual connection and Energetic expansion that is more than we could ever had hoped for. As DZAR says, we are all in the space of becoming more of who we really are as an expression of the light, joy and essence of All That Is. They tell us that there is no separation between us and Spirit, even though it feels like it in our limited perception of reality on this plane, and this is the message and the experience they are here to share with us all.

Our first meeting with DZAR

It was only sometime after our first conversation with DZAR, that we realised that DZAR's Energy had been trying to make contact with us for some time. That story begins in America's Sangre de Christo Mountains nine months earlier.

We were in a small town in Colorado called Crestone, staying with our dear friend and the originator of the PSYCH-K® processes, Rob Williams.

Crestone is a spiritual centre and home to many different Buddhist, Hindu and alternative centres all coexisting peacefully together protected by the powerful Rocky Mountains and overlooking the San Luis Valley. It is an eclectic community where almost everyone is involved in mystical or metaphysical practices. I remember one day going with Rob to the post office to collect his mail, and as we were walking back to his car he exchanged greetings with a guy who was one of the local tradesmen. As we drove away Rob said, "You know, that guy is typical of most of the people who are drawn to Crestone because as well as being a local tradesman he's also a healer."

While we were there, Gary booked a massage with Marcia, a local healer who also worked with guides and spirits. I was a bit surprised as it wasn't the kind of thing he would normally do and the only time she had available meant he'd have to miss out on another activity that had been arranged. But he felt very strongly that he was meant to have a session with her.

As he lay on the table, he began to realise that this was no ordinary massage. He could feel her massaging his head, while at the same time "someone" was at his feet massaging his leg. Then as she was massaging his right arm, he saw a very clear image of himself as a warrior preparing for battle. Thick leather armour was being fitted to his arms and he knew that this was his final battle, and that he wouldn't be returning to his family but that he had a duty that he must fulfil.

After the massage, as Gary stood to get dressed, he noticed that his legs felt very weak and shaky. He went through to the kitchen where Marcia was waiting for him.

"That was a powerful session," she said, "the room was filled with guides and energies and they said they were taking you to the next level of consciousness."

As he heard her words, he began to sob. The tears were uncontrollable and although they weren't tears of pain, at the time Gary found it hard to describe the intensity of the emotion which lasted for three hours. It was only later on reflection, that he was able to recognise them as tears of relief at having reconnected to these Energies.

I had booked a session for the next day with another local mystic, Juelle, who channelled a group of energies that gave spiritual readings. Rob and other friends had been to her and recommended her highly. I was going to see her hoping to gain clarity about why, despite all the personal change work I was doing, I still felt blocked from moving forward in my life.

She welcomed me to her home overlooking the valley and I sat comfortably in a deep chair as she prepared to connect to Spirit.

It was a lovely Energy that came through and spoke with me, leading me through a number of clearing processes. In one of the processes they took me through, I walked through a doorway and came out into a large green field, with a brilliant blue sky and sunshine overhead. There waiting for me, was a group of Spirit Beings. It was an emotional and joyous reunion as they told me they'd been waiting for me to join them for a long time and they were so pleased that I had connected with them again.

At the end of the session, Juelle told me that the removal of the blockage I felt was holding me back would be complete by the time we left Crestone that same day. I was elated and felt deeply moved by my experiences with the group of Energies that had greeted me so warmly, and I was excited to see how my life would be different.

Beware of expectations!

It had been a powerful time in Crestone for both of us and we didn't really know what would happen next. We'd both reconnected to powerful Energies and so we both expected that there would be changes in our lives. We thought that these would happen within the work we were doing at that time; perhaps we'd experience more flow, or some 'lucky' breaks would come our way. Little did we know that those experiences would unfold into our connection with DZAR and the message they have asked us to share with others, as it was nearly 12 months later that DZAR first spoke to us using Gary's voice to channel their message.

Looking back on that year between our time in Crestone and our first conversation with DZAR, there were many signposts along the way that gave us clues to the presence of their Energy around us. But because we were expecting the changes to happen within the format of what we were doing, we were looking for them in particular ways and so we didn't really pay attention when they happened.

A funny one, that I remember clearly, happened as I was sitting and meditating one summer's day. I was alone in the house and before I began, I asked for a sign that I really was connecting to Spirit during my meditation. As I sat on the floor, focusing on my breath, the central heating suddenly came on....in an otherwise empty house...in the middle of summer...

It gave me quite a fright because deep down I wasn't really expecting a sign, so I sat there for a moment and then got up to check the controls. Maybe they'd somehow been bumped earlier that day and the switch had flicked on, which would explain to my logical, rational mind what was happening. But sure enough, the controls were still turned off, so it seemed this *was* my sign from the universe! The heater hadn't been used for some months and it had never in the 4 years we'd lived in the house turned itself on...all on its own...until that moment...

Given DZAR's sense of humour, I'm sure it was them 'turning up the heat' to get my attention! I told Gary about it when he came home, but as it didn't fit with the kind of guidance or communication from Spirit we were expecting we dismissed it as a funny anecdote. Had I been more open and less fixed in what I was looking for and how I thought it would happen, I would perhaps have recognised it as a sign that Spirit *did* want to communicate with me in some way and I would have pursued this overture further. As it was I ignored it, so it was another few months until they were able to make contact with us again through the channelled writing process we'd learnt....and you've read what unfolded from that!

As DZAR says, "When you connect to your Expanded Being, you will hear the messages from your Soul if you allow them to be present without restriction. But when you place a particular way upon it that it *should* be, you limit your awareness when it is presented and you wonder why Spirit doesn't listen to you. We think it is more that you don't listen to us, so it's lucky we are not easily offended!"

Conversations with DZAR

This is the first book in the series **Conversations with DZAR**. It offers an introduction to the message that DZAR has been sharing through their talks and the workshops we run with them.

It includes a special Meditation that you can download from The Path of DZAR website (www.thepathofdzar.com/book1) and also Practices that you'll find in the Appendix to support you to re-experience your Expanded Being, the term DZAR uses for your Soul, and to reconnect to the compassionate Energy of All That Is.

As you read the book or listen to any of the talks that DZAR gives, you'll notice that the way they communicate with us is both profound and at times very moving, while also being quite humorous. Some people on the courses have been a little surprised that an Energy from All That Is could have a such a cheeky sense of humour when DZAR calls people nicknames, or 'threatens' them with the universal harpoon! This may be because many of us have been brought up in faiths where showing respect has been interpreted as having to be serious.

But as DZAR often reminds us, this is the path of joy and so the humour, the banter and the jokes they use with such compassion when they are talking with us, are all part of the light and playful frequency of All That Is. And this also explains why people feel happier as they experience a deeper connection to their Expanded Being on this path of joy.

Chapter 3

Understanding the Journey
of Your Soul

Welcome back, Young Ones, this is DZAR. We hope you enjoyed Mary and Gary's story and can see its relevance to you as you begin this conversation with us. It is an important piece and we ask that you take a moment now to reflect on your own journey of becoming.

Sit quietly and reflect on all of the twists and turns in your existence that have brought you to where you are now in your life, to the synchronicities and chance meetings that have been Spirit supporting and guiding you back to living as your Expanded Being.

Can you see the times when Spirit was there to guide you but you perhaps missed it? Can you feel the times when you moved forward in your existence connected to your Expanded Being and how differently things turned out for you? Was there more flow, more joy in your experiences?

As you move forward in this conversation with us, stay open to more synchronicities and 'coincidences' being present, for they will become a normal part of your days when you are connected to your Expanded Being and able to hear the messages from your Soul.

We have heard your questions

Those of you who have been in front of us have asked many questions, for you want to understand the reason for your journey, you want to understand the experiences that have shaped your life. In this part of the book, Young Ones, we will answer your questions; Why am I here? Why have I been put into this place at this time? Why has my life been this way? Is there something more? Am I something more than I think myself to be? Is my Soul needed for this journey? What is a Soul, an Expanded Being, a Spirit? When I have no hope left, is there any hope for me?

There are so many questions about this journey that you are on and you have asked many questions before, but in everyone's life there comes a pivotal moment when your questions are answered and your change truly begins. For those of you hearing these words and feeling the Energy of our answers, that time is present with you now. You are asking these questions not from a space of being superficial, you are asking these questions now from a deeper internal, more expanded space for this is where you wish to be, this is what you wish to feel.

We have heard you asking these questions across lifetimes, and we feel your earnest desire to understand and to shift your experiences, to become more and to be the light for yourself and others on your planet. So let us answer them for you, and you can then share your understandings with others, for that is your role as an in-lightened Being.

So let us begin to understand some of these expressions. The story of your journey so far, the story of your Soul and the messages it has to share with you.

Your true essence is always present

Many of you experience the difficulty of returning to your essence because over many existences you have allowed your experiences to become a part of you. You have allowed aspects of the pain and the fear of these experiences to become your identity, to become your sense of Self, you have allowed all these things to become who you think of *as* you. What they indeed do, is place an Energetic field between who you truly are as an Expanded Being and who you think you are as the Constricted Self and so therefore you feel that your current experiences of living are real...and we know that for you, they certainly feel real!

You originally came forward with a clear Energetic space, as a pure expression of the Energy of All That Is and your purpose was to experience life in each existence connected to your Expanded Being. For it is through experience that both you and the universe expands, it is how knowledge becomes available for all. But within some of these experiences overwhelm and personality began to cloud your true purpose and connection. They started to come between you as a complete expression of your Energy and you as an earthly Being, and so the separation began.

In your early existences, you could easily reconnect to the sense of your Expanded Being but over time you began to connect more deeply with your experiences, you began to identify more strongly with them and you allowed the gap to grow. Through many lifetimes, through many experiences the juggling act has continued between your Expanded Being and your Constricted Self.

Now you have come to a space in which you feel a deeper connection, an urging to reconnect to the true you. And there are times when you can still reconnect to this space, are there not? Times when you feel its joy and flow present. It is all the space of allowing, it is all the space of releasing now whatever is in your path so that you can be the complete expression of the true you, of your Expanded Being. For this is what we have heard you crying out for, that is why there are many of us here on your planet at this time giving you information and ways to reconnect again.

So if you were to begin with the fact that you have not forgotten who you truly are and that there is only a gap, a bridge for you to cross, then what does this feel like? If this feels more do-able, more acceptable then that is how it should be.

Your true essence is always present, it is always with you. It is always wishing your expression of Self on the physical plane to be the fullest expression of your Expanded Being for, as we have said before, this is your purpose. This is how you become a teacher contributing to the changes on your planet just by being you, by reconnecting to that light within you, by crossing the bridge and by reducing the gap through each existence until there is none. You will then light the way for others to do the same, for others to live their physical lives in full connection with their Soul.

That is how community begins, that is how community expands, by you being the light that others follow, for not judging yourself or another as to how they presently are, and by accepting your connection to all things. When you do this, you are compassion itself and by allowing yourself and everything and everyone else that surrounds you to be in this space of becoming, you allow these things to manifest in whatever form and in whatever time they take. There is no rush, there is no deadline, for you are always expanding and it is a glorious experience for you all.

Your Expanded Being and the Constricted Self

To continue on your journey, we want you now to move to the awareness of yourself as an Energetic Being comprised of two parts; the Energy of you that is eternal, and the Energy that is only present when you are drawing breath.

You all exist with the Energy of the in-lightened Self, which we refer to as an Expanded Being, at your core. This Self is the reflection of All That Is, with the compassion of the universe itself expressed within it. The Expanded Being is the fullest expression of your Soul, of your true spiritual nature; it is the Source Energy of creation that exists within you.

The other Energy that is a part of you is a limited or constricted form of the Self. It is an expression of Self that has been battered and bruised by the pains of past life experiences. We call this the Constricted Self. For many, this is who you know yourself to be in your current form and it is why you are asking the question that there must be more. For even while you live in the experience of the Constricted Self, you can still feel the expansive Energy of your Expanded Being within you, seeking its expression in your physical existence.

So let us understand them both, let us begin with where you are now and please understand that there have been times when you have felt an expanded sense of who you are, you have felt a stronger connection to the true compassion of the universe in this and other lifetimes. But for many of you those times have been short-lived, and it is what you are wishing to experience more of, for you can feel its presence deep within you, even as you read these words, can you not?

The Constricted Self is the culmination of all of the different expressions of you that have gone before in your past existences. It is shaped and formed from the experiences in those past lives that you have held on to, that you have taken on as *being* you. It is the sense of Self you have brought forward from lifetime to lifetime, and it is made up of all the experiences from your current and past existences which have been misunderstood so that only a partial understanding or learning was received from them.

The Constricted Self is also a reflection of your environment, which includes your family, your society, and of course the planet you live within. When you look at the world through Constricted

Eyes, you create your environment and your experiences of pain, so it is both a filter and a mirror for your experiences.

From the Constricted Self come the many labels you place upon your experiences. The labels of right and wrong; good and bad; the way forward seems difficult; the way behind even harder; the sense of now is confusing. These labels of your experiences and the ways of being attached to them are so familiar to so many of you that they have proven difficult to give up, difficult to be free of because who will you be then? You do not see them as separate to you, you do not recognise that they sit around your Being constricting and limiting it but rather you think of them *as you*. You know yourself so well in this form because it is so familiar to you, and this familiarity keeps you stuck, this sense of knowing who you are from the constricted space keeps you right where you are.

You look at the world and your life through these Constricted Eyes and you only see more of the pain and separation that you have known so well. For so many, the thought of moving forward from the sense of Self that you are now feels so arduous to attempt that there seems little hope that you can expand into a brighter Being.

But you *can* move forward, Young Ones, and in fact you are already moving forward as you read this book and feel the frequency of our message. The more that you connect to your Expanded Being and feel its frequency, the easier and faster your journey forward will be.

The Expanded Being is the space of awareness and it is the experience of connection. When you look at your world and your existence through Expanded Eyes, you see the sameness in all things, you see possibilities, you feel compassion and you experience the guidance of your Soul. It is your awareness of your connection to who you are, it is your awareness of your connection to what is around you and how that too is a part of you. The Expanded Being is the space in which the true reflection of the universe exists, the reflection of compassion, compassion for Self and for everything that surrounds you.

So it is always your choice, your choice to look through Constricted Eyes and stay with the familiarity of your Constricted Self or to shift your sight to your Expanded Eyes and head into the unknown of your Expanded Being.

But is your Expanded Being really unknown, for how can something unknown feel so familiar to you? If you could not feel your Expanded Being, Young Ones, you would not be asking these questions, you would not be seeking ways of reconnecting to something larger. We find it amusing that you are looking for something more expansive, more powerful that you think exists *outside you* when in fact it exists within you and that is where your search must begin!

Your Expanded Being is your guiding light; it is the alignment of your Energy, your chakras, your meridians and any and every other name you wish to understand it by. It is a force that flows through your entire body that connects to everything and to everyone. It is universal, it is ever present and it does not ever diminish. It only ever expands and it is always moving you closer towards us. It knows the way home to who you truly are, and it is always guiding you back along that path.

Take a moment now to complete the **Expanded & Constricted Eyes Practice** at the end of the book so that you can feel the difference between these two expressions of Self and see how you create your experiences from them.

You are Spirit incarnate

When you live as your Expanded Being, you live in the awareness of yourself as Spirit incarnate. When this happens, you know yourself to be so much more than your physical existence and the experiences contained within it, but you do not discount them for you understand the role they play along your own path of expansion and learning. So you embrace *all* of you and you live as the fullest expression of Source Energy as you can in each moment, you live as Spirit and physical Being combined.

Yet for so many of you, this is not how you experience your existence. These two aspects of Self seem to be separate and even incompatible, yet it was not always this way. So let us start at the beginning of your journey, let us go back to the very first time you left us, to understand how this has happened.

Your first physical existence

When you first left All That Is to experience a physical existence, you left as the purest expression of your essence to experience life on the physical plane. You came to experience life as a human being, all the while staying aware of and connected to the true Energetic expression of your Soul. You wanted to live in the knowing of yourself as a spiritual Being having a physical human existence, recognising the difference between the two expressions of your Energy, while experiencing their sameness without any sense of separation between them. The planet these early Souls came to was perfect for this adventure, for it was created to give physical expression to the Energy of your Soul, to the frequencies of compassion, of joy, and connection with other Beings and with all things.

You knew that the only way you could have experiences was via a physical form which is why you took on the shape of the body. You were a young Soul wishing to grow and expand through the experiences on the physical plane. As a young Being, you had not yet gained your own wisdom and you became distracted by the excitement of the wonderful physical manifestations of Energy you encountered. And as you did, you became less aware of your Energetic Self, less aware of your connection to your Soul.

When you first came to this planet, you were like a child in a sweet shop. You found the new experiences of your physical Self so delicious, so enticing that you wished to have more and more experiences, to try everything, to sample every sweet in the shop, even if a stomach ache was part of the experience. For it was all experience and you enjoyed it all, for that was why you were here.

You enjoyed the way you were growing in your physical existence. But because you were becoming less aware of your Energetic essence and becoming more identified and focused on your physical Self, when it came time to release the physical experiences, to let go of the experiences of pain or loss, it became harder and harder to do so. You had always wanted to *have* physical experiences and see them as separate from you, but you had begun to identify with them. They were now how you saw yourself, they had become your expressions of Self, your personality in that existence, they had *become* you.

It was the accumulation of all of these experiences which you took on *as* you that created the original separation between your Soul and its physical expression on your planet. Your physical Self became limited and constricted in its expression and in its connection to your Soul, it became the expression of Self you think of as you during each existence. It became the Constricted Self.

So when you left that first physical existence and returned to All That Is, you understood what had happened. There was no judgement in this space, for you were a young Soul on your journey of existing as a Spiritual Being on the physical plane and this was part of your growth and learning. So you decided to return for your next existence with those expressions of Self and the experiences you had become so attached to. You decided to return with them so that you could release them and live in that existence in full connection with your Soul.

This was not a punishment, it was not a hardship for your young Soul to return in this way, for you wanted to grow and to achieve your original goal of living as both a physical *and* Spiritual

Being in each existence. So your Soul returned with the same level of connection – or disconnection – from your physical experiences as when it left.

In the early stages of your planet, as a young Being, you may have experienced small pains if you hurt yourself, you may have felt some form of emotional pain but it was so new, so exciting, so tempting that your did not avoid these experiences. But as you moved further and further from your connection with your Soul and identified more and more with the physical Self and with the experiences of pain or loss, these experiences became a part of who you thought you were. And because you *are* Energy and your environment is a reflection of you and you are a reflection of it, you began to reflect more pain into your environment and therefore you experienced more of this pain as you.

As more and more Beings did this, the Energy of your planet began to change, its original frequency of compassion, joy and connection was still present but now it also included the frequency of pain, of loss, of suffering, of separation.

Every time you descend, you experience many things. And if you become attached to the experiences, if you forget who you really are *in* the experience, then these experiences become deeper expressions of who you think yourself to be. When you allow the pain and the fear of these experiences to become you, you allow them to shape your very form, you allow them to materialise in your body, to shape the complexion of your face, to control your metabolism and the ability to heal within your own body. This is what happens when you lose connection with who you truly are. This is how the experiences become you.

You were always meant to experience and to live your life in all its richness, but you were *meant* to live your life connected to your Expanded Being so that while joy and pain may be part of your existence, you experience them in vastly differing amounts to how you are now.

Your Soul connection as a child

You sense that you forget your true Self but, as we have said before, you do not truly forget. You are a Being who when born feels your true essence, you know who you are and you can sense so much more of the world than many of you do now.

When you are a young child, you understand that there are two selves, two aspects of you. There is the one you feel so strongly inside of you, that is so familiar to you. This is your eternal essence that you bring forward from existence to existence, it is the part of you that you know *is* you, for it is your Soul. And then there is the one which feels new and unfamiliar, the one that responds to the touch of your parents, that smells the smells of your outside world, for it is your new physical self in this existence.

Many of the younger forms perceive their essence as an imaginary friend, and it is a friend but it is not imaginary. It is your Expanded Being and it is very real for, even though you cannot touch it in your physical world, you can feel its presence so strongly within you.

When you arrive in your new existence, you bring with you the awareness of your true essence so that you will have a familiar friend to talk with, to hold, to feel safe with. You stay in this remembering of your essence when you are young, and then when it is time for you to begin your own journey and to have the experiences you have chosen when you were here with us, your remembering of your Expanded Being fades.

When you are in this space, you see so much for you do not see things only as the physical form that they are, but you also see and feel the Energy of all things. Many talk now about children who have been called Indigo*, children who have a greater awareness of who they are. And we would say to you that *all* children are Indigo in this meaning, they always have been, and it is a name that was

---

* Referring to the term spoken of by Kryon, an Energy channelled by Lee Carroll.

brought forward so the adults may recognise that there is something special about the little ones in their care. For all children come into the world with this expression, with a depth, with an understanding, with a seeing that is different to many of those who have come before.

So do you wonder why, if children have always been this way, it is only now in your times that you are aware of their special ways of being? Do you wonder why it is only now that books are being written to help all to understand it? If it is not *they* who have changed then it must be you, the adults, who are becoming more aware of this frequency, this essence of All That Is inside *yourselves* so that you can now feel it in the little ones. For without awareness of this essence within you, you cannot feel it or experience it in another. It is why we have said that the change always begins with you first, for that is key to your expansion and to experiencing this Energy in those around you.

As you grow as a little one, you begin to identify more with the physical world and less with the world of Energy. For remember, you have brought with you the expressions of Self and levels of disconnection or connection to your Expanded Being from previous existences so that you can learn and grow. So you begin to understand and form a sense of self that fits into your family and environment whilst attempting to stay connected to the expression of Self that you were when your friend was present, for that is always your goal. And we know that many of you have not found this an easy thing to do.

So, Young Ones, the more you become connected to who you truly are, the longer your friend will stay with you in each existence, until you and your friend can journey through every existence together. It is not that you need to be the child again, but you seek to experience the child's truth within you, you seek to experience that sense of connection, to experience a world in which there is no separation and you are the complete expression of your true essence.

The understanding of the young child is the understanding of the Expanded Being. As a young child it is indeed the time in which you have been closest to your Soul, so treasure that space, allow yourself to reconnect to it and celebrate it when you see it in the little ones that are around you.

Experiences and the Energetic Cloaks they create

During your existences, Young Ones, there have been times when you have experienced pain and struggle and you have remembered who you are and have chosen to transcend these experiences. You have seen them as "not you", as being transient and separate from you, so that you were able to stay connected to your essence even in the midst of the experience.

And there have been those times when you allowed yourself to be consumed and lost in the experience, so that your true sense of Self was diminished and you have felt abandoned and alone. When this happened, you became stuck in the Energy of the experience and you began to see the experience *as you* and, because you now saw it as a part of you, you continued to manifest its Energy in various forms through out your life...and through out many lifetimes.

We have called these Energies "cloaks" because they cover your light, they create an Energetic barrier around your Being so that it makes it more difficult for you to connect to All That Is. They make it more difficult for you to remember yourself as the frequency of compassion and to live your life *knowing and being* the Energy of creation.

Let us look at an Energy that has been taken on, an experience that you now think of *as you*. The primary role of that Energy was for you to feel the experience, to understand it as *not you* and then to release it. But so many of you begin to wear it proudly, so many allow it to cloud the true light that you are. Over your existences, this is how you have created your current shape, your current identity, your current knowing of Self.

You have created yourself from energies and expressions you

have taken on so that you have become them and they have become you. It is very difficult in this space to exercise what you believe as your free will, where you believe that you have choice and we are sure that many of you have experienced times in which you feel you have no choice at all. This is the expression of your current Being; this is the expression of your current sense of the Constricted Self.

The space of the Expanded Being is the space where you begin to get in touch with the Energy that surrounds you, the space where you can choose any experience with awareness, understand the role it is playing in your expansion and then release it. That is the expression of awareness and true free will that an Expanded Being has.

It is not that you resist everything, for you are Beings of experience and that is why you are present. There are indeed some experiences you would certainly like to leave alone, and the interesting piece is that you can. You can also dwell in them for a brief time and then release them, rather than allowing them to become a part of your current existence and living through them for many lifetimes.

There is no separation

So many of you feel alone, you feel separate, isolated and disconnected. We want you to know that you are not alone, for you have access to Energies inside and outside of you that are waiting to support you to live a life of joy and connection with all things.

It is time for you to remember that you are part of something much bigger than the physical body, much bigger than the consciousness and the environment that you exist within. We know that many of you have forgotten how to tap into that expanded sense of Self and to live from the space of the magnificent Being that you are, and so we have brought forward processes for you to learn to do that again.*

Your essence is the frequency of compassion. This is also the true frequency of the universe because you are the same, there is no difference, there is no separation. As you release these cloaks, these aspects of your Constricted Self that are restricting you from feeling and *being* your essence, you will merge back into that boundless sea of compassion and begin to experience the joy and abundance of all creation. You will know yourself to be expansive and infinite, you will know that you truly exist outside the dimensions of time and space that have created the illusion of separation and limitation.

As you reconnect to your Soul's magnificence, your life will change, for how can your Soul feel pain? How can your Soul feel loss or separation? How can your Soul not recognise its connection to all Beings and to the earth you walk upon? Of course, it cannot.

Each time you end an existence and return to us and to All That Is, your remembering and your knowing of who you are returns. You merge back into All That Is and re-experience your pure essence, your light, your unbounded majesty. It is now your time, it is now your choice to live in this experience of your Expanded Being in every moment.

That is the possibility that our message brings you; to reconnect to your essence and experience each moment of your human existence from this place of knowing that you are not your experiences, of knowing that you are boundless and that you are a perfect reflection of the compassion of the universe. For that *is* who you are.

---

* DZAR is referring to the processes in the online Learn to Channel the Wisdom of your Expanded Being course.

Chapter 4

You Create the Universe

Now that you know who you are, now that you understand you *are* an Expanded Being which resonates with the frequency of compassion, we wish you to understand the role you play in the universe. For what does it mean that you are not separate? What does it mean that you are an Expanded Being connected to the essence of All That Is? So, Young Ones, let us begin with an expansive view and then we will bring the information down to a compact enough size so that you can understand your part within it.

The universe is an expression of Energy

You exist within a universe that is an expression of Energy. It exists to support life in all its facets and, through this, to express its true frequency which is compassion. All life forms are unique, on your planet and on others, and they are part of the grand design, for they all are expressive Energies whose core frequency is also compassion. Their purpose is to expand into this awareness and be an expression of this Energy across the entirety of space. As this expansion of compassion occurs, it creates an equilibrium in the frequency that is being transmitted by all forms. Once balance is created and compassion becomes the strongest, clearest frequency in your universe, then new life will begin to form from this expression, from *your* expression. So you see, as you connect more to your Expanded Being and to its frequency of compassion, you become the Energy of the universe itself.

The universe is always heading towards harmony. Its main purpose for existence is to be in a harmonious state, everything in balance, everything perfect. In the same way that all Beings are in the space of becoming the fullest expression of their essence, the universe is also in the space of becoming the fullest expression of its frequency of compassion. Your universe is not static, it is evolving and expanding in response to the energies of the Beings on all the planets that contribute to the frequency that it is.

In this space of becoming there are times of imbalance, times in which life forces of all types are still understanding who they are and their connection to the universe they exist within. Everything that is present is connected and has a form of awareness. You are not separate because you are made of flesh and the grass is not. It is all life, and all life is connected to all things, all life is a part of creation, and it is all a part of the universal plan of balance. The overall goal of creation is to have all forms of life living in harmony with each other, to have all systems coexisting on a balanced plane. Is this obtainable? Yes, it is. Are you an integral part of this mission? Yes, you are, Young Ones.

If there is to be true harmony in the universe, the dominant frequency must be compassion, for harmony between all things cannot exist otherwise. That is why your journey is to reconnect to the essence of your Expanded Being and All That Is, for their frequency *is* compassion. As you live from that expanded connection, you expand the expression of compassion on your planet and across the universe so that all may feel it.

You are the Energy of creation itself

The moment you recognise that you are not different to this Energy of compassion and creation, and that you have the same expression as all the other Energies that you have made worthy to be your idols and your gods, then you are moving along the right path to being the fullest expression of your Expanded Being. Within the compassion of your Expanded Being there is no judgement, within this compassionate space there is only embrace, there is no sense of feeling separate, no sense of feeling sorry or better than. Compassion is the purest expression of Energy there is, it is a oneness which is all-accepting and embracing of another and of all things.

When you *are* this frequency, new life will be formed from you. You cannot see yourself as an individual to understand this, you must see yourself as the holistic expression of the universe. It is your Being that resonates with a frequency that is the same across all Beings, across all living creatures upon all planets. For you see, each Being interacts within another no matter how many light years apart you perceive yourself to be. The separation and distance you perceive is just in the physical form. Energy and matter are not separated by time and space, they coexist, there is no distance. That is only a viewpoint from a linear Being caught within the illusion of its physical form. And you are recognising yourself as so much more than that now, are you not?

As you grow and expand, Young Ones, your Energy is felt by other Beings on your planet and by other life forms millions and millions of light years away. When this happens, your resonance and their resonance join to create a unified field. This field is the expression of compassion which is the true Energy of the universe, and the more life forms that begin to gain awareness of their compassionate field and to live from that space, the faster more worlds will be created, for the compassionate field *is* the Energy of creation.

If the Energy that you are has a direct lineage to creation itself, then you must play some part in it, and your existence must have a grander meaning than you are aware. For you are not a separate Being living a singular existence whose only connection is to the family you see. You are an Expanded Being, one of deep consciousness, one of deep resonance, one that is sensitive to the Energetic ripples both near and far, both in your world and the next. The ground you walk upon, the air you breathe, the world you see, the space you imagine, are all created from exactly the same stuff as you. You are a part of it and it is all a part of you, so there is no separation, there is no difference.

So it is a grand plan, is it not? And it is truly a magnificent moment when you fully accept the Being that you are and the role you play in the creation of the universe.

Your role in the expansion of the universe

There are those who have the view that there is no point to you being who you are; that the meaning of your existence is as simple as your 9 to 5 job; that the extent of who you are only exists as far as you can drive your car or peddle your bike; that you are separate, that you have no connection to anything else. This would seem a rather random and pointless way for a universe to exist, would it not, to create life for no purpose, for it to trundle along on its way, generally sad, never truly merry and then to become dust?

Or there is the other understanding, Young Ones, where you *know* that you have a purpose, that your life has meaning and connection. You know that you are not just a fluke of evolution but that each life has meaning. You know that you extend much further than you can peddle your bike, that your eyes can see so much more than what is in front of you and that your Energy is everlasting and connected to a greater whole.

It has always been for you to decide which it is. We know that eventually you will all see who you really are and the role you play, and then you will know that your life, your existence is not a game, it is not an experiment. And at that time that you know this, you will make an important contribution to the creation of the universe purely by the shift in your frequency, for that is how worlds begin.

We know that many of you despair, you watch your news and it feeds the continual images of pain and separation on your planet and so you believe that this is how your world exists. But what you don't see, is that there are many others who live in the world with a sense of Self that is also starting to stir, a sense of Self that is also starting to hear the inward call. The change is happening, the Quickening is upon you, and you are part of its creation.

You do not need everybody to make the shift but when many do, the others will shift. It is what you call your critical point, where more and more Beings are beginning to feel the true essence of creation and compassion that they are and they are allowing that to be their expression with each breath they take. The more you live from this space, the more you will find it does become contagious to those next to you, for it stirs the Energy of creation within them, it becomes the dream for their awakening, the catalyst for their change. And as you begin to feel a deeper connection to the one beside you, the space of compassion and community grows, and the experience of separation from each other and from your true Self is transformed.

As the Beings and the frequency of your planet move closer to the frequency of harmony, to a shared experience of compassion, it begins the creation of more life; it begins the manifestation of a more expansive field. This is your contribution to the universe, to the creation of worlds, for as you become a clearer expression of your Expanded Being you shift the frequency of your planet and the universe expands.

Chapter 5

You Are Beings of Energy

When you are first born, as the purity and compassion that is the Energy of All That Is, it is like a star being born and there is a light that shines throughout the entirety of the universe and is reflected throughout all the worlds. This light continues to shine through every day of your existence, never diminishing in its brightness so that no matter how old your Being is, you are able to see and reconnect to the magnificence of that Energy, of *your* Energy.

This Energy is the expression of you right now. It is who you are when you return to us because even with all the expressions and experiences you have faced, you still return as the brilliance that you were when you left the first time.

There is a great movement of magnificent, compassionate Energy that is happening around you every moment, yet there are so many who do not feel or sense its presence. Your Soul, your Expanded Being is the ticket to you experiencing that magnificence every day, for the purity of that Energy is within you and so your journey is to be that, to remember it, to expand upon it. That is your purpose for being here. Your physical form has a Soul for that is the device that makes you whole, it is the Energy that is the true reflection of Self and that has the memory of all creation within it. It lives within you and so you *are* this magnificence.

Your essence is eternal

Your essence, once created, once released from the true source of creation is eternal, ever-expanding, ever moving forward. So, just because the breath leaves the body that you currently inhabit, do you not return to another one to continue your journey of experience and expansion? The Energy that inhabits the new physical form is your eternal life, it is your Soul, it is the aspect of you that is ever-expanding, ever-experiencing. So how can there be two Beings the same? There have been so many different experiences in your lives that you have accepted as you, that go towards making up who you currently are.

So let us have a conversation on this point, and let there be time for you to dwell upon this point of you having an essence that is eternal.

What would your sense of Self be if you knew this to be so? If you knew this not from the level of your mind saying, Oh yes, DZAR I know I'm eternal, I've read that before, but from the level of deeply knowing and feeling this in your Being?

Take a moment to reflect on this. What would your sense of Self be if you *knew*, as your Being knows, that the physical frailty that you may currently be experiencing is only within this aspect of time and will not be present in the next? If you *knew* that it was an experience for you to be grateful for? That it is an experience where understanding, not resistance is required, so that you do not *become* the experience. How would your existence change if you allowed the essence that is within you to be your guide through such a time, knowing that in the true wholeness of your time that this life is truly short-lived?

You are not your experiences

The understanding of yourself as an eternal Being *right now* is essential to your acceptance of who you truly are. It is from this view that you can begin to see how so much of the character and the traits that exist within you have been brought forward by you from previous existences. When you see this, you can begin to understand how it is that you are who you are now, you can understand how you have connected with the family, the friends, the situations that you currently have in place.

When you see your existence from this space, you see the perfection of it all. You see how in each experience that you have chosen there is an opportunity for you to connect ever more deeply with your Being, rather than connecting so strongly to the experiences themselves. For that is your goal, to know that *you are not your experiences*, to know that you are not the pain and suffering you have endured, that you are not the experiences of limitation and restriction that hold you back. And while you are in the knowing that they are not you, at the same time you accept that they are yours. You know that you have brought them forward from many previous existences so that you can transcend them, so that you can see them as the manifestations of your Constricted Self. When you know this, you can then expand beyond them through your stronger connection to your true essence, to your Expanded Being and release them from your future existences.

For the understanding of true consciousness is that of acceptance and awareness. An awareness of who you have been and an awareness of the future that lies around you. An acceptance that you are eternal and that you are greater than the physical form and all that it contains. An acceptance that your knowledge of Self is a key component to you living a life of fulfilment and joy. It is you living from a space that is exuberant, of *being the space* that is aware, that sees through Expanded Eyes the magnificence in the small and the majesty that is connected with you. For the whole purpose of you living this existence is for you to see your own magnificence and to be connected to a space that never ends.

You are the frequency of compassion

Our purpose is to reunite you, to help you to remember the essence that lives within you, that essence which *is* creation itself. This Energy that is in every cell of your body, is the generator that fires the spark of creation. Understanding that this spark is a part of you is certainly important, but knowing and accepting that *this spark is you* is your purpose. If you could accept this, imagine what your life would be like then.

If you *knew* that you were creation, that the very essence that manifested the world around you was living within you, within your body, within your Energetic field, what would your life be like then? What would your sense of Self be when this was known? Would the way that you walked through life be different? We would think so. Would you be more supportive of who you are, more compassionate? We know so. Would the way in which people were attracted to you, the way in which they relate to you be different to how you experience it now? Of course.

This space is present for those who wish to listen, it has been awakened because you have asked for it, because you have felt deep within you that there must be something more, that the space you currently exist within is not a true reflection of who you are. You know this, Young Ones, you feel this discontent, this unease that lives within you, you feel resolute in changing your conditions and because of this we have become present to your needs. We are here so that our words, our frequency will mingle with yours to help light your way on your journey home. And when you do, you will then begin to light the way for so many more who have yet to be awakened.

Your first step is to know and accept that you expand further than the extremities of your skin, you must know that you are a Being that is Energy, that is expansive and connected. Then as you connect to your expansiveness, you will begin to understand your position on this planet and your position within the entire universe. You will accept the fact that the very Energy you *are* creates change across the entirety of space, that you are not a singular Being, that you are a Being of amazing power. Your ability to tap into this space and become the Energy of creation that others will wish to follow is your purpose upon your path through all your lifetimes to come.

If you were looking for your true purpose in all your existences, then there it is. Your true purpose is to be the essence of creation, to know that you are the compassionate Energy of All That Is and to allow it to glow from every pore of your body. To know in each moment that this *is* you, that you are Source, that you are Spirit as you walk in the steps of compassion. For this is who you are, Young Ones, this is who you have always been. It is now your time to live in the knowing of this.

It is time to release the experiences from all your past existences that have held you back, the fears that have laid you dormant from your true purpose. It is now time to become the star that others look towards. It is your time, Young Ones, it is *your* path. We are here, we are waiting and ready for you to ask for direction so that we can help you find the light that *is* you, the same light that is us.

And it may be that as you read these words you are wondering if we have problems with our memory, as we seem to repeat ourselves in this book! But just as you read the message from a love one over and over again and know them off by heart, the messages from your Soul that are written on these pages are repeated throughout our conversation so that you feel them resonate deeply within you, until you remember them for yourself and hear them as your words for that is what they are.

You are an expansive Energy

Some of you who are reading this book are feeling that you are not the words that you are reading, you do not feel yourself to be the expression of the Energy of All That Is, connected to all things. Then let us present you with some information that may indeed lead you to being more aware of just how far you extend already.

You are not separate, you are always in communication with both the Self and the environment around you. As we go through this next section, we wish you to remember the times in which these spaces of expansion and connection have occurred in your life. And as you do, you will begin to have the awareness and acceptance that maybe you are more than the physical Being that you think you are.

First of all, let us consider that your body and your mind are more than just flesh and blood, that they communicate with more than just your physical form and that there are many aspects to your current form that extend far beyond the physical space you exist within. For those of you who are in a relationship, consider how many times have been present when you have had a thought and, without speaking a word, your partner or friend has expressed that exact thought. How does that happen?

How is it that when you are unhappy, your world seems to place other unhappy events in it, from the stubbing of your toe upon a table that you have passed many times before without incident, to being stopped by every red light on your way to work? So it seems in these times, one bad experience occurs after another. Then you receive a message that shines light back into your day, and does not the day flow smoothly from there? Perhaps it is words of love from someone you care for, or some special message of great meaning to you that transcends the pain you have been experiencing. You feel the frequency of love or compassion or joy in those messages and it indeed shifts the whole physicality of your Being. From that moment, you perceive only flow in the remaining hours of your day, you experience ease and the world is a different place for you.

Can you remember these times? If you are purely a physical,

separate individual how do you explain them? How can a change in how you feel in your body influence the things that happen around you?

If your life is just flesh meeting flesh, how can these things be? If indeed the way you are feeling, the sense of sadness as one expression, the sense of happiness as another, can create such different occurrences in your day around you, how can that be? Are they not just feelings? Are they not just emotions that you feel only within yourself? How do these expressions have an outward experience in creating your day?

Can you begin to accept that there must be some power attached to your expression of Self for your Energy to change the world around you in these ways? And if you begin to accept this space, can you begin to see how far the emotions you experience internally, affect your world externally? How far beyond your current form do you think they extend? To the person beside you and to everyone you seem to meet in that day, or even further into areas that you are not even aware of as you move through your day?

For you cannot see the ripple effect of your Energetic existence, you cannot see how far your frequency extends. When you take this time to place your awareness upon the events of your day, you will begin to notice how far you extend. Now, let us take this another step.

Your body is Energy

If this is happening around you, what is happening within you? When there is the feeling that you are constantly under attack, that you are experiencing stress or disappointment in your life, does your body reflect this, do your thoughts reflect this, do you tend to be sicker than those around you? Do constant problems of the physical form tend to haunt you? You may indeed eat all the right things, take all the right pills, but still the imbalance seems to be present. Can you begin to understand the picture that is being painted?

You are indeed an Energy Being having an Energetic experience through the physicalness of your body. If you can begin to accept these facts, you can begin to accept how you create who you are in each moment. Look upon the size and shape of your own body, how often do you marvel at its form, at its majesty or how often to you criticize and judge what it is you see? If everything is Energy, can you understand why your experience of your body is the way that it is? In this existence you judge bodies as one form being better than the other, but they are not. You have had many forms and shapes through your existences and, depending upon your society at the time, you have revered a larger form and scorned the thinner frame or vice versa.

Many of you have *become* the reflection of the judgements of your society. It is time for you to be the reflection of your true Self. It is time for you to accept and to understand that your thoughts and your feelings have frequency and form connected to them, that your body and your environment is a direct reflection of how you are feeling about yourself, of your level of connection to your Expanded Being. They are a direct reflection of who you think yourself to be, of your expression of Self, for it is all created by you.

So take a moment now and view your body from the space of your Expanded Being. View your body through Expanded Eyes, marvel at its creation, celebrate its intricacies, be compassionate with all of its expressions. See it as the perfect Energy of All That Is in physical form.

Do this now, Young Ones, and then with awareness, notice how your body feels, notice what happens to the aches and pains or to any aspect of its experience that you do not enjoy. Can you feel the changes? Do this as a practice, as a daily way of *being* your physical Self and allow your body to be in the space of becoming the true reflection of your magnificence.

Your expression of Self creates your reality

Now take this awareness further, and reflect on which aspects of your life and your relationships are an expression of your Constricted Self. Notice how they are the expression of a Self that feels separate, that feels limited in its expression.

Now look on those areas of your life that reflect the expression of your Expanded Being, the areas in your life where you feel expansive and connected. Look at those areas where you know yourself to be the creator of your existence, where you feel the compassion of your essence and of the universe that surrounds you.

And we know that you will be experiencing both aspects of these in your existence, Young Ones. You will know of times when you feel your true expansive nature and, though they may be fleeting, though they may seem to be outweighed by the pain of separation from your true Self, they *must* be present. For how else could you be asking the questions that are bringing you back into connection with your Expanded Being and your true purpose in this existence if they were not?

So if you can indeed reflect upon the simplicity of what we have said, then you can accept who you actually are and you can become aware of the reality you are creating. With expanded awareness, you can step onto a path that will lead you to where you truly wish to be, to the space of an expression of Self that is whole, for that space is within you right now. Once you begin, you will be guided along it and you will create your existence from this space in this and all future existences.

For you are always creating your existence, Young Ones, and the difference will be that you are beginning to create your existence from the space of awareness of who you are and what your life is all about. You are always in constant communication with the world around you, you are always expressing in each moment who you think yourself to be and the world reflects this back to you, it is that simple. What we suggest, is that you express yourself from the space of who you know yourself to truly be, from the space of connection to your Expanded Being and allow the world to reflect that back to you and then rejoice in its expression.

Your current existence is the expressions of all your lives past, you are the current amalgamation of each life lived. You have continued to move forward through each expression of existence into a fuller form of Self, but many of you experience this existence through all the cloaks of the pains and the doubts that keep you separate from who you truly are. The environment is reflective, it reflects your expression of Self back to you through the experiences you attract. The misunderstandings and difficulties you have in this life are definite signposts to old expressions of Self you are not releasing, to new expressions of Self that you are not accepting.

If you believe yourself to be an individual who is different and separate from all the rest, bigger and better than the one next to you, less important or less worthy than those around you, then they are all expressions of past life experiences that you have not understood and released. They are all expressions of your Constricted Self, for they are all based on the Energy of separation and difference, and in those experiences there is no space for compassion.

Celebrate these experiences, Young Ones! For if they are occurring, they are signposts along your road towards the final destination of you living your existence in full connection with your Expanded Being while enjoying your physical life on this plane. If you do not see when a turn sign that will move you closer to your destination is present and you keep driving, you end up where you do not wish to be. You can do this over many lifetimes, Young Ones, for it is always your choice which direction you take in each of your existences. So have awareness and follow the signs that you have placed upon your path, for they are there waiting to guide you home.

Chapter 6

Living Your Purpose

We know that many of you wish to find your life's purpose, for you feel that when you find it all will be well, all your problems will be solved and all of your questions answered. So you will be pleased to know that it is there to be found...as long as you are looking for it in the right place, and we have given you many clues already in our conversation with you. But so often you begin by looking for it outside of you, you believe your purpose is related to what you *do* in your life, the work you pursue, the businesses that you run.

Your purpose is not about what you *do*, Young Ones, but it is all about *who you are* in each moment of the doing, it is all about your expression of Self and the level of connection you have to your Expanded Being in everything that you do. So that is where you must begin your search!

Your life's purpose

From the illusion of separation, you reconnect to your essence and you begin your awakening. That is your purpose, that is why you are here. This was a short chapter, was it not? But let us explain further and share with you a practice for experiencing this for yourself.

You are here to be awakened, to connect with the light that shines within you so that you can *be in-lightenment itself*. This is your purpose in each and every existence that you have ever had and in those still to come. For when you live from this space, you contribute to the expansion of all Beings on the planet, you contribute to the expansion of compassion on this planet and across the universe. What greater purpose could any Being, any Energy have!

Does this all sound rather selfless to you, Young Ones? A noble cause perhaps, and yet you may be wondering where is the mention of *you* in all of this? And that is a fair question, for we know that many of the religions on your planet seek similar outcomes. But the Energy of the Messenger is interpreted in many different ways, and some have determined that a path of sacrifice and suffering is required to create this result. So there are many tales of martyrs and the inflicting of torture for those who have sought to expand the compassion on your planet. It is a curious interpretation, is it not?

We hope you have not forgotten that The Path of DZAR is the path of joy! So the only things we suggest you sacrifice along this path are your limited expressions of Self, for they are the very things that will keep you separated from the joy you seek. This is the path where you can experience the true abundance of the universe, where you are in-lightenment itself living in the expansive and joy-filled space of compassion and connection.

When you understand that your purpose is to live *as* the in-lightenment of your Expanded Being, you will begin to see the world through Expanded Eyes that have no boundaries or judgements, you will experience an expression of Self that is truly expansive and wishes to experience everything that your world has to offer.

But DZAR, if there are no boundaries, will I seek experiences of pain for myself or will I inflict physical or emotional pain on others?

Of course not! For why would an Expanded Being that is the living expression of compassion, seek experiences such as these, where is the frequency of compassion in such actions? When you live in connection with your Expanded Being, you will only seek experiences that will expand and deepen your connection to All That Is and you will only take actions that will contribute to the unfolding of that connection in others.

Your Expanded Being is already in-lightened, that is its expression and it is the expression it seeks to share with others so that they too may live in this space of joy. This is how you were always meant to treat yourselves and others, and this is the space that so many of you are wishing to return to.

Sit quietly for a moment, Young Ones, and feel the space of your Expanded Being; notice how expansive it is; notice how connected you feel to who you truly are and to all things around you both seen and unseen. It is a magnificent experience of being, is it not?

Take time now and reflect on what your experiences would be like if you did not place judgement upon them, if you could release your perceptions of what has happened to you? What would abundance mean for you then?

So that is your purpose, Young Ones, to live as the compassionate Energy that *is* your Expanded Being so that others may experience that joyful connection as well. It is the same for you all, but because each Being is a reflection of all of the experiences it has had throughout many existences, the way you live out your purpose is unique to each of you. And that is where the fun begins for that is a question you must still find the answer to and you *will* find it when you are living your life from this space.

Become the Practice of the Expanded Being

You have already experienced the Practice of the Expanded Being that is at the end of this book, and we wish to speak more about its true power coming from you seeing it as a practice that you *become* rather than an exercise that you do.

The space for you to begin is to be compassionate with yourself in this space of *becoming* your Expanded Being for this is a practice; it is the way of you becoming the entirety that your Soul can be. Each day and each moment, you become the Practice of the Expanded Being, moving forward step by step until you reach the space of your true in-lightenment in this physical form.

Understand too that you do not need to wait until you reach the ultimate goal of living in full connection with your Expanded Being. From the moment you decide to journey on your path, your light begins to fill the space and it will only ever grow in its intensity as you continue to release the Constricted Self, the Self that is not reflective of your true essence. As you do this in each moment, those around you will feel your expanded Energy and it will be contagious, for as others see the smile upon your face that has replaced the frown, they will feel the reflection of your Expanded Being and they will be drawn to it. They will want to experience it in you, and they will want to experience it in themselves.

The more you *become* your Expanded Being, the more you will reflect the light that you truly are. You will begin to experience more flow and ease in your existence, you will find the moments of pain to be shorter, and fewer the experiences that manifest that pain. From your connection and the awareness of your Expanded Being, you will see experiences that may contain pain or hold the potential to limit your expression of Self coming towards you. You will feel them in the distance and you may choose to allow them to pass you by or, with your awareness, you may also allow them in to visit. But when you are connected in an expanded space, the way in which you experience the situation is different, for you are experiencing it from the viewpoint of its overall meaning in the expansion of your Being. You are viewing it from the space of your growth and therefore the way you experience it will be different.

If it is an experience of lack, of not experiencing the fulfilment or abundance you seek in a situation, you may allow yourself to experience it briefly, you will understand how it has been manifested from the limited expression of your Constricted Self and you will release that limitation and any attachment to the experience.

You will not take the experience on as you, you will not see it as more proof in your life that you are unworthy or that the world is unfair. Instead you will see it as an experience created by a limited expression of Self and you will learn from it and then release it. When you do, your Being will become more expansive, your connection to your light will become stronger, and you will move forward into experiences where fulfilment and abundance are your reality.

The importance of steps on your journey

We know that many of you want change instantly, that you want *all* of your pain to go away and for your life to be magically transformed from this moment to the next. And depending on the changes you are seeking, Young Ones, they can be instant and many of them will unfold as *a series of instant changes* that are spread over time.

You are an Energetic expression that has manifested over centuries, all of the aspects of Self that you currently experience have become a part of your field, they are a part of your organs and your cells. If you were to change *all* of these aspects that are so much a part of you instantly, it would be as if you dropped a bomb in the middle of a populated city...the fallout could remove innocent bystanders.

When you first begin living as your Expanded Being in connection with your Soul, it is a very special time for you. You have existed within an Energetic field that has kept you in a specific state for many lifetimes, so when you begin to release this Energy it is important not to rush the process. It is important that you begin to feel the Energy again, to experience your Being, to experience the light of All That Is within you, a piece at a time. For as you can understand, if you were to release this space too quickly it would overwhelm the Being. It would be like you jumping from being a young child impatient to grow up, to suddenly being an adult. The changes to the sense of Self and your connection to the people and the environment around you would be so extreme that there are few of you who would be able to stay in this new space.

We do not believe in bombs and we do not like you jumping straight to the end, because your reconnection to your essence and to All That Is, is a process, it is a journey. It is you reconnecting to the Energy of your Being and it must be grown and nurtured as you do with all other things that exist within your planet. We understand that you wish to get to this point quickly because you have endured the pain for so long, but if the Self is not in a space that can sustain the changes then you will soon fall back to where you were.

Remember, Young Ones, your purpose is to have experiences so that you can learn and expand through them. It is the pain of the Constricted Self that wishes to avoid them completely and jump to the end but your Expanded Being does not want to miss one single step. When you are connected to your Expanded Being, your reactions and your responses are so different, and the experiences you attract into your life will reflect your true frequency and they are experiences that you will wish to savour. When you do this, the journey which you now wish to avoid becomes joyful.

Do not hear this as a path of struggle and effort, Young Ones, for it is not. When you are in the space of becoming your Expanded Being, the journey along your path is one that is filled with joy as you experience life so differently, as you experience yourself in so many new and wonderful ways. So why would you wish to miss one step?

Imagine yourself as someone who was good at running when you were a little one at school, and now as an adult you wish to run in the big league. You are needing to train, you are needing to support your mind and your body for this challenge. From the space that you are beginning now, to that time when you reach the ultimate goal of running in the big league, there is a process, there are steps, there is no jumping from where you are now to breaking that time barrier.

Think of what you will learn along your path as you train and prepare to become the kind of runner you wish to be, think of how you will come to understand your mind, think of how you will learn to work with your body because in each moment you are wishing to improve, you are moving towards something you desire. You know that this process takes commitment, dedication and time and through that practice comes great satisfaction and fulfilment.

There is no difference, Young Ones, to you training to be a runner or to you becoming your Expanded Being. The process is the same, you must release the fears and restrictions you have about yourself, you must accept the challenge that lies before you, you must put your focus on what you want, on being the kind of Being you wish to be and then in each moment *become* more of that.

And, because this is a practice and you are in the space of becoming your Expanded Being, you may experience days that you would not call joyous, you may experience days when you do not feel as expansive as you wish. But you know that the end game is much bigger, and so you move through whatever life delivers you so that you can experience the fulfilment of living as your Expanded Being, connected to the compassionate Energy of All That Is.

It is a process, it is a practice that you do every day, it is an expression of Self that you *be* in every moment. For how can this level of change happen in any other way?

The problem with your free will

This is always your choice, Young Ones, because Spirit will never make you do anything, we will always allow you to choose the next step along your path.

We feel your heartfelt desire to reconnect to your essence, and yet so often you use your free will to make choices that keep you trapped in this limited expression of Self. Does this not seem strange to you? Do you wonder why you are at times your own worst enemy?

To understand this, you must recognise how free will is expressed by many of you.

So often you take actions that keep you separate and limited because your decisions and actions are filtered through your cloaks, they are expressed through the Constricted Self. So while you think you are using your free will, it is the free will of the Constricted Self trapped within its doubts, pains and limitations. You are making choices based on the aspects of your past experiences that you now think of as you, that have held you back through many, many lifetimes.

We do not call this free will, Young Ones. True free will is exercised through your Expanded Being as you listen to the guidance and messages from your Soul, it is not filtered or constricted by your past experiences or your fears of the future. True free will is exercised from the wisdom of your Soul, without fear or doubt, it is always guided by your connection to All That Is.

Feel this for yourself now. Think of a decision you are yet to make, and become aware of the choices you think you have. Become aware of the feelings associated with the different options you are considering, the expression of Self within those situations.

Now take a moment to connect with your Expanded Being

and become aware of that decision and the choices open to you now. Are they the same? Do you feel the same about them? How is your expression of Self different now? Will one of these paths will move you to a stronger connection with your Expanded Being while the other may keep you in the space of your Constricted Self?

It is always your choice, and we wish you to make your choices from the space of your Expanded Being, from your connection to your expansive Self which will guide you and protect you as you move forward. For you know the experience of the Expanded Being better than you know your current Constricted Self. When you are here with us, that is who you are and when you are living your human experience, the Expanded Being still exists within you. It is still a part of you, for it is your true expression of Self even though you may not experience it greatly in your day-to-day existence.

The Expanded Being is your Soul, it is the reflection of your eternalness of Being, it is the one constant that is ever present, it was there when you began your journey and it will be there when you end your journey. Your whole purpose is to come back home to us as the fullest expression of the Expanded Being and you do this by living your purpose as an Expanded Being while on your planet.

Imagine a world that is filled with such Beings living as the expression of universal compassion, living in the universal awareness of who they truly are for the majority of their existence. Imagine a world of Beings where the frequency that they display to their outer and inner world is one and the same, compassion for Self and compassion for others and for all things.

We know you have explored these thoughts, we know that you have wondered how they may be possible and we want you to know that this is not idle imagining on your part. That is why you are reading these words, it is why you are moving so strongly towards your own connection with your Expanded Being because you can feel it resonating within you, seeking its expression for your expansion and growth and for the growth and expansion of compassion on the planet you exist upon.

We understand from your current position, from the familiarity with your Constricted Self, this seems easier said than done! And that is why we are here, for you have called us forward, Young Ones, so that we can support you to make this change, so that you can move from the limited expression of Self to the space of living as the joy-filled expression of the true Expanded Being that you know yourself to be. We call this The Path of DZAR and as you read this book, as you have been engaging in this conversation with us, you will have realised that The Path of DZAR is the path of YOU. For like us, you are an expression of the same Energy of creation, like us you are truly an expression of the compassion of All That Is, for we are all one and there is no separation.

Chapter 7

Your Return To All That Is

At the time when you return to us, when you are at the final moment of your existence, you remember again who you truly are, you feel the compassion of your Soul, you feel the true sense of home. You know in that moment the essence that lives, that has always lived, within you and there is a peace that descends upon the body so even though the physical form may feel the pain, it is never left in that way.

No existence is ever in vain

In all of the existences that you have lived within, not one lifetime has been in vain, not once has there been a wasted experience, not once has your Being not grown or expanded in some way. Even if you only existed for the shortest time, every existence, every experience has purpose and meaning for the expansion of your Being. The way you were in the space of that existence was all so right for who you were in that time.

Even when the heart stops its beating, the body is laid to rest with the memory of the compassion of the universe and of the magnificence that you are in its cells. And so you leave the body that has been your vehicle in that existence and you return to us. You return with all that you have learned and all that you have not learned and it is the time for rejoicing, it is the time for you to be bathed in the true light that you possess, it is a space of comfort, it is a space of the ultimate experience of your true expression.

The space of true awareness

When you return to the compassionate embrace of All That Is, you reflect on and understand the meaning of all your experiences in that existence. All the perceptions, judgements and resistances you had while you were in the physical form disappear, and you are left with the awareness and the understanding of the Energetic expressions of those experiences. You understand the love and pain that you experienced and how they have each contributed to the expansion of your Being, how they have played their part in you reconnecting to your essence while on the physical plane. And there will be times for all of you, when you became attached to experiences, so you will also see how these responses held you back from your connection to your Expanded Being, how they kept you feeling separate and limited.

In your next existence, you choose to have experiences with a similar frequency to those you became attached to, so that you can stay connected to your magnificence and release the frequencies from your Energetic expression of Self. You do this because your goal is to be able to live in a physical form of existence where there is no separation between life and death. When you reach this level of connection, your form of expression is the same on the planet that you exist on as it is within the plane of true compassion here with us. It is possible, there are many who have done so and there continue to be many moving towards that fullest of expressions.

So, if you can feel your Soul resonate with this

understanding, if you can feel the connection to the true purpose of your Being, the question is why wait any longer to live in this expression of Self? Why wait for some future existence to live in the day-to-day connection with the Energy of All That Is and the compassion of the universe, why wait for a future existence to feel that frequency resonate through every action you take?

If you feel these words within you, if you feel their resonance, then you are in the space of quickening your journey to being the fullest expression of compassion itself. For can you not feel that the plane you live within needs such an expression to be present? That is your role. You are all sages, you are all the ones who, upon realising and *being* this Energy, will reflect the light upon those next to you so that they too may have the realisation that you have had. You then become the reflection of the god; you then become the reflection of the universal expression of light and compassion. That is your purpose, that is why you are eternal, that is why the expansion continues.

When you release your body

Let us discuss then the space at the time of death. As you have already read, there is, in that moment, the time when the body and the Spirit are in true fact reunited completely, where the body that you are releasing is reunited with All That Is. That is why we have said that in that moment you leave that ever-lasting sense of compassion with your body, you make peace with it and in that moment you accept it, you thank it for its journey with you.

In many ways, you have an Energetic conversation with it about the wholeness of your journey together and you leave the body in the space of peace. It is not left in pain no matter how it died. It is important for you to know this. The expression of you that was contained within the flesh is released, it was a part of the body and it contained the essence and the understandings that you will need in your next existence. In that moment, you share a pure experience of compassion. For no matter how you may have felt that your body treated you, in the moment when you leave it, all of the understandings and awarenesses are taken on to your Soul to be brought back to the expression of All That Is.

We say it is the true moment of compassion, for it is the one true moment of complete acceptance; it is the one space in which Energy and flesh are completely in acceptance of each other. It is truly a beautiful space. Yet imagine if you did not have to wait until your death to experience that magnificence, what would your life be then? How expansive would your experiences be then?

This is the space of you coming full circle, for there are times when you were young, as we have said, when you remember where you have come from and you again know exactly who you are just before you leave that physical form. So there is just the small bit in the middle for you to connect up!

So with that expression complete you return to us, you return as a fuller and more compassionate Being than when you left. In this moment you feel so alive, you feel the fullest connection that can be experienced. In this space, you are embraced and the conversations that are had are ones in which complete acceptance is always present. It is a space where judgement does not show its face. Imagine the communications that take place in a space such as this, in a space where awareness and acceptance are the natural ways of being. You can see that from this space an Energy can only grow, it can only expand and blossom. It is the one space that you never truly forget and it is the one space that you are always wishing to obtain when you are in the physical form, for it is truly what gods are made of and you are made of this.

In this space of complete compassion, you also understand what it is that you need to move forward and aid your own growth in your next existence. You are told the answers to your questions across all realms of your existence and you continue to build a story from which you will read when you are in the physical form. This story is filled with the messages from your Soul that are there to guide you through your experience, they are waiting for you to turn the cover and begin reading.

Your time with us is to replenish the pages of your story, and this is why we have always said that you have the answers. You know what it is that you must do to expand, to be all that creation is because it is all in those pages, in the pages of *your* story.

The space of acceptance

More of you are doing just this, more of you are reading the messages from your Soul from the pages in your book. You are starting to fill in the pieces of who you truly are. More of your memory, as some of you call it, is returning but it is not memory that is returning, it is the awareness of what you already know that is becoming known and accepted. Your time with us when you leave an existence is not something that can be measured as long or short, your time with us is measured in what it is that you need to be and accept to move into the next existence and continue the expansion of you.

In this space, there is acceptance of everything that you wanted to do and did not. So each time you return to All That Is, you are indeed doing many reviews of all your lives, accepting them and understanding where each piece fits. For you are always moving forward, you are always becoming more expansive for that is how your Being learns. The more your Being accepts the understandings from its existences, the faster you move into your next existence and so the faster you expand. For you must understand that every Soul is different, every Soul is in its own space of becoming its fullest expression, so there are different rates of acceptance for each of you because you are at different frequencies on your paths of becoming.

The earth is a giant learning space, it is where you create who you are. Through each existence and through all your experiences, you are expanding as a piece of All That Is, your frequency and your Energy are growing. Your experiences are different from the one next to you, so you may think of Souls as individuals, for they are indeed a collection of frequencies based on the life experiences of each Being and what each one has understood about them. So you are unique, and yet when you are present with us, you recognise your sameness to all other Souls. You feel the commonality between everything that surrounds you in that space, and you do not feel separation because all frequencies are contained within the expression of All That Is.

And there will be a time, when you will live in that feeling of the sameness between your Energy and the Energy of all other Beings when you are your physical form. When that happens, a different turning point will occur upon your earth, a different expression will begin to grow because of that frequency. This is still a little way off in your terms but you are moving towards it, becoming closer to this space through your connection to your Expanded Being and your acceptance of who you truly are.

When you live from this knowing, your life and the experiences you have will not feel so serious because you will experience in each moment your true purpose to expand your sense of Self through your acceptance of your experiences. When you do this, you will know that you are eternal and that this life is but a brief moment in your true history.

Chapter 8

You Have Lived Many Existences

Let us now speak of the space of you understanding your past lives and the aspect of why you do not remember them, why you do not remember who you have been in physical form.

You are complex Beings in so many ways. You have all lived many, many lives and you have experienced many things. These things that you have experienced have become who you are today, they are the current expressions of you, they are as real as the flesh you know to be yours. The expressions of lives past are the expressions of your present life for there is no separation in time or space.

The meaning of your past lives

The memories of your past lives are signposts. They are signposts that you have planted along your journey so that you can revisit them to gain an understanding of how your past experiences have contributed to your expression of Self in this existence. Your reason for understanding them is not to cling to them any more, not to become lost in the pain of past existences, but to understand and to release them so that you can become a fuller expression of your Expanded Being in this and future existences.

In your pasts, many of you have experienced much pain. If you were to reconnect to that pain again from the space of separation from your Being, it could very easily take you to the edge of an abyss that you will not wish to visit. It is one reason why you cannot remember everything that has happened, it is your own self-preservation. That is why when you look back from the space of your connection to your Expanded Being as your guide, it will allow you to see the experiences but it is not necessary for you to feel the disharmony of those experiences, for that does not serve you. You do not need to re-live or re-experience the pain of past existences to gain an understanding of how those experiences have contributed to your expansion or how they have held you back.

The alchemy of the universe

When you are connected to your Being, you can gain awareness of those experiences, accept the role they were intended to play in your spiritual growth and release your attachment to them. When you do this your Being expands, the Energy of those experiences is released back into All That Is and it is transformed into the Energy of compassion and so the universe expands. This is the alchemy of the universe, for it is through your release that all experiences are transformed into an Energetic substance which is more valuable than the gold you prize on your planet.

Many who have gone back to experience past lives have received different answers and we wish you to have awareness of the expression of Self that is asking the question, that is seeking the experience. If you ask the question from a space of separation from your Being, from a space of fear, from a space of wishing to fill an empty space within you with some fantastic story to give your life meaning, then you will more than likely uncover a misguided past experience. Your current limited expression of Self will guide you towards it and it may make an intriguing story. But, Young Ones, it will not contribute to the release and expansion of your Being from these past experiences, for you will still feel your attachment to it, you will still feel connected to the pain or the drama of that story.

Then there is the other way, to ask from the space of the Expanded Being. When you ask from the space of a Being that is already whole, from the space of your own eternal compassion and you move back through your history from that space, you will see and understand more about how you can move forward in this lifetime so that you can be your fullest expression of Self now.

From this space, it matters not who you were in your previous lives. Knowing if you were a great leader or a simple farmer will not serve you moving forward. It matters not who or what you were, what matters are the aspects of Self that were manifested in that life. What matters is how closely you heard the messages from your Soul.

If you were attached to your experiences in those lives, if you took them on and saw your failures and triumphs *as* you and made them part of your identity, then you will have created the experience of separation from your Being. They will be holding you back in this life as well, for they are creating the separation between your Energetic and your physical Self, they are the expressions of your Constricted Self. You can create separation whether you are a great king or a humble servant, so it is not who you are that matters, that is not what makes you great. What makes you truly great is when you understand and release your experiences in each existence and you become a clearer and stronger expression of the magnificence of All That Is and contribute to the alchemy of the universe.

This is the value of understanding the circumstances of your past existences. With your awareness, you can choose to release any attachment to the experiences from those existences that are holding you back and move forward into a new beginning in this existence.

That is the space to explore your past existences, for it will support your growth and connection not just to your own Being, but to all Beings on your planet as you see the sameness that exists in each of you beyond the labels of your identities.

You are a Being of wisdom

Many of you think of your past lives as times of torment and torture. You think of yourself as having been burnt at the stake, as having suffered and lost all that was dear to you, and for many of you these have been aspects of your past existences. But not one Being living on your planet has only experienced pain in an existence. You are all Beings of wisdom, you are all Beings who have an understanding of how to move forward, of how to live and there have been many, many times in each existence where joy, connection and compassion have existed because of the expression of Self that you were in that life. The frequencies of these experiences are present with you in this existence now, for you also bring those expressions forward with you into each future existence.

There have also been lives in which you only experienced flow, a sense of ease and movement that was present from one breath to the next. There have been lives for some of you, in which when pain approached you, you were able to see its path and move aside or to allow it brief entry, understand it and release it again with complete acceptance of why it was present. For this is how awareness becomes useful, this is the space of the Expanded Being, a Being connected to their true essence and to All That Is.

When you *are* this way of being, then even the pain is not pain because that is a label that is placed upon it by those who do not understand it, by those experiencing it from a limited expression of Self, from a space of separation from their Expanded Being. When you are in the space of the Expanded Being, you know that pain is an experience just as happiness is, that it is all Energy passing from one expression to another and that they are what you are here to be a part of. And, Young Ones, we understand that you may wish some of them to linger longer than others! And so they will, for the more you live as your Expanded Being, the more you will exist in the frequencies of the experiences that you find pleasing to you on this physical plane, for how can you live in joy otherwise!

Claim the joy that is waiting for you

Yet so many of you do not feel these existences of joy within you now. You only feel so strongly the pain that you think has been etched upon your Soul, though nothing is truly etched upon your Soul except the joyful expression of your essence. You feel this pain, because the strength of those expressions of joy, fulfilment and compassion that are present is dependent upon how aware and accepting you are of your true essence in *this* existence.

The more you reconnect to your true Expanded Being, the more you will feel the expansive expressions that you have been in previous existences and the more you will share your light and your compassion with those around you. At the core of your Being you know this to be true, you can feel those expressions of joy resonating deep within you seeking their release, seeking their expression in this existence. And as we have said before, Young Ones, that is the reason we are here, for you have called to quicken the process, you have called us forward to assist in your expansion and your reconnection to the joy and compassion that is your true essence.

So if this message resonates with your Being, go back and claim the happiness that you know is yours. Be ready to accept the joy, the love, the connection from previous existences with open arms, without criticism, without any sense that it cannot be present in your life now.

It is acceptance and awareness again. Awareness that a life lived in joy is something of your own creation, something that you wish to experience again. And acceptance that the space of pain, or the perception of it in this life, is no longer required for it is not the true expression of you.

With acceptance and awareness, you can reconnect to that sense of joy that you know *is you*. Do not discount the true power that lives within you, for once you truly experience the joy that has filled your past lives, it can flood this existence and reconnect you so quickly to your true Self again.

Do this now, Young Ones. Be still and connect to your Expanded Being, use the Meditation we have provided for you with this book and allow the light of your Soul to guide you back to the joy that is waiting for you. Once you have made this decision, you are on the path of your in-lightenment for you know it is time to re-experience joy and to be that fullest expression of you now.

You are on the path of your return, do not allow your perception of time moving too slowly to work against you. Do not expect for everything to disappear in the blink of an eye, for if you do then look at the Self who is asking and wishing that to be present. Your decision *will* bring you home.

You are on a journey, you are in the space of becoming the fullest, truest expression of who you are. Your life is one of deep meaning, of deep expression so experience it from this space, Young Ones. You are now the one ready to shape this existence and those yet to come, to be the captain of your own ship and this time instead of a sailing ship, it may be a star ship that will return you to your own universal essence that gives birth to galaxies.

Chapter 9

A Community
of Compassionate Beings

Community, Young Ones, is a way of being, it is the true expression of Self. Community can only be present through the expression of compassion, and compassion can only be present through the direct connection of the true Self, for compassion is the highest expression in the universe. It is the understanding of everything being created as equal, as all having the same essence so that there is no separation. It is the understanding that the Self is connected to all things and to all other Beings.

Take a moment to consider what your concept of community is and also how far its expression expands across your existence. Do you have an experience of community within your own family? Is there a sense of community *within you* for everything that you are?

Is there the sense of community that is expressed in the place in which you live? Or do you feel alone? Contemplate these questions for a moment, feel what is brewing within, think of what your expression of community is, feel what your experience of community is.

Is community something you do or is community something that you are? And where indeed does community begin? We hear you say, DZAR, we know what you're going to say! Well done! We are happy to state the obvious that community begins within you first. What does this look like? What does this sound like? What is its true expression?

Take a moment now and reflect upon these questions, and when you are finished begin to read again.

Community is the expression of compassion

Community is the expression of compassion. Community is created by Beings like you who are connected to their Expanded Beings and who radiate this frequency into the world around them.

From this space, the light that you *are* invites others to join you without the use of words, without the use of a physical act. It is purely the Energy that you are, from that space of knowing yourself to be a Being of compassion connected to the Energy of All That Is. You allow this Energy to flow towards the one beside you, towards those around you and to all you cannot see, for you now know that you are more than just this single space. You now know that you can radiate the frequency of compassion that exists within you across the entirety of your globe and you can feel the presence of others who are doing exactly as you are. This is how community begins and you may need a larger space at the special festive times, for you will have such a large, extended family to invite to your table!

Imagine an expression of community from this space,

coming from Beings that know who they are, that know why they are present in each moment and whose connection to all things radiates nothing but compassion towards all Beings. When this is the feeling within you towards your own sense of Self, your deeds are those which in each moment are drawn from a compassionate Self. The true love you have for you is always reflected within the world that you see and so is reflected back again to you.

Of course, we are not talking purely of the physical act of community, we are talking of community as an Energetic expression based on you understanding that you are more than the physical Being. Community is not the physical act of having a large group of friends present in front of you, though for some of you this may be the expression of community in your existence. For those of you who understand you can heal someone without actually seeing them, that you can send someone love without actually speaking the words in front of them, you will understand how you can be a hermit and still display so much love to the world that you are known by all and seen by none. The great mystics of your time have understood this space, you do not need to be known to be felt. It is an important piece to understand.

You create this Energetic expression of community because it is the direct reflection of who you are *being*, it is not something you do to seek recognition from others. It is created from the space of your Being, the frequency that you are creates a ripple effect of compassion that others feel and resonate with also. When people feel your presence they may offer you the physicality of a smile, yet you have done nothing, you have just stood there in their Energetic field and they have felt your Energy. In that moment, you may have presented them with something so valuable that it changes their existence forever, for this may indeed be the first time they have truly felt love without any judgement attached. In that moment, their exploration begins of how they themselves can be this expression.

At the physical level you will not know if you have indeed done this, but at the level of true existence you know that it is the way of an in-lightened Being to create more light, more connection, more compassion and more joy in your existence and on your planet for others. And you accept it as that, for nothing more is needed.

Global consciousness is created through community

The shift in global consciousness is the shift of Beings expressing their expansion and compassion to their community and connecting with the very soil they are a part of. They are the switches, the lights that will turn on the others. Global consciousness is only created by groups of Beings like you, Young Ones, connecting together as community; it is created by groups of Beings projecting their Energy out so that others may feel this space. For when you are your full projection of Self in community, you can turn the switch for those who are still in the space of remembering, for those whose awareness is just beginning.

On this planet it is a time of rebuilding, you are currently seeing the expression of a place that is uneasy, you are currently seeing the expression of a planet that is feeling it is not wanted. It is now time for you all to begin to show your true expression and to rejoice in the changes you will create as a connected community of in-lightened Beings.

Chapter 10

Your Connection To Your Earth

So, Young Ones, as you have been reading this book, you are beginning to understand the true aspect of Self that lives within you all. By now you may begin to feel that warmth of the Self that is true. It may still indeed be small and yet it is there. This realisation is a frequency, it is a vibration, it is a resonance, it is how we communicate with you and how you communicate with us. It is from this space, from this understanding that we now ask you to turn your eyes downward to the earth you walk upon, to the soil that supports your life and to the planet you live within.

You live within your planet

Gaze upon the earth beneath your feet, and now turn your eyes upward towards the sky that provides the light, the warmth and the water that also sustains your existence. We are talking here, of course, about the planet that you live within. And we deliberately say that you live *within* your planet rather than upon it as many do, for you are within its Energetic field, you are within its frequency so there is a deeper connection than simply seeing yourself as existing upon its surface.

It has been your choice to incarnate upon this soil; it has become your mission to live out your existences within this space. In doing so, you build up an impression, a unique frequency impression, within the Energetic field of your planet that flows into the soil that you stand upon, into the air that you breathe and the water you drink. Your frequency resonates with the earth itself, it feels and hears your heart, it knows your Soul.

The planet you live within, which many refer to as Gaia, is also a living thing, it also communicates, it also resonates and it too has a purpose. There is the space of sameness that is spread across the entirety of the universe, the sense of connection between everything, and there is also the connection between you and your earth for it cannot be any other way.

Your earth absorbs and reflects your Energy and it will support you based upon how you support it. It feeds back to you your own frequency and thus far you can feel how the earth you walk upon treats you because of who you are. And in this current moment, it is not as happy as it could be and that is all based upon the reflections it is feeling from all that live upon your planet.

The Earth's reason for being is your reason for being. You have chosen to be upon a planet that has awareness, that has connection to your Being that is also expanding its frequency. The earth that you walk upon is the energetic reflection of you.

You are the best fertiliser there is

The more of you who know this fact, the more of you who realise that you have this deep connection, the more quickly your earth will change. For it is not just about adding organic fertilizer to a soil, that is so superficial! You are the deepest fertiliser for your planet, you are the heartbeat of the earth you walk upon as it continually feeds back your frequency by the way you connect to each other, by the way you feel about yourself. The earth responds to all of this, to your expression of Self and your expression of compassion to yourself and to others.

You are all looking for the causes to the current situation of your environment, you are seeking solutions but you are not seeking them in the right places, Young Ones. We hear you say, Oh but DZAR, it is all about science, that is how we will fix our problems! Is it? Science is how you attempt to explain what you are doing, science is how you try to make sense of why the weather is changing as it is, why the soil and your crops are both diminishing. But why do so many of you feel less connected to your land than in any time in your history. If you are not connected to the land then what are you connected to? Can you see the separation you create? You place a distance between each other, you place a distance between you and the soil at your feet and then you sit there and think that it makes no difference. Time to think again, Young Ones.

If you *knew* you were connected, if you deeply felt that connection, how would you treat the earth then? If you knew that the person next to you was the same, how would you treat each other? How would that combined vibration nurture the earth? Can you see the cycle, can you begin to understand how it works? You are all living things existing together, seeking harmony and, in this current time, there is still the separation. You have distanced yourselves from the traditions that connected you to the land, and in doing so you destroy the air you breathe, the forests, the soil, the oceans and you forget who you are.

Change your expression of Self first

If there ever was time to change it is now, if there ever was a time to have a consciousness about who you are, about what you do, about your connection to the earth and to each other it is now. It is not about you trying to cut your emissions because look at the falsity that has been created by this bandaid.

You created the emissions because of your Energetic disconnection from the earth and you will all drive electric cars to make things better, but the cause is still there! You are still disconnected, you still do not care, many of you still think the earth is an inanimate object, you think it cannot feel the frequency of you. We say these words in a firm manner because it is time for you to hear them, Young Ones, it is time for you to step up to the plate and change who you are because the earth will listen, the earth will respond because it is connected to you. That is why you are here, that is why we are here to help you reconnect and for the earth to flourish once again.

The earth you walk upon and build your homes upon has had many, many expressions over its time. Its Energy is never still; its expression is ever changing. Yet you look upon the land and you see the same hills, the same trees but so many of you do not see the Energy that it emits. It is like a giant radar that captures signals from the inhabitants of your lands and then transmits them back to you. So the first thing to work upon is your own expressions, to begin to accept that connection that you have to everything. Then live as your Expanded Being so that the earth can feel your reconnection to the frequency of compassion, your reconnection to the Energy of All That Is that is the Energy of creation.

You can do this now, Young Ones. Go outside and lay upon your soil and allow the Energy of your Being, the compassionate frequency of your Soul, to soak into the land. Feel its gratitude as it receives this gift that only you can give to it. Send the deepest expression of your essence, of your Soul, the frequency of your Expanded Being into Gaia, into the one who supports you, allowing it to feel your new expression and compassion of Self.

The more of you who do this, the more your earth will begin to respond differently to those who walk upon it, the more you begin to realise your own expanded field.

So take the actions that you believe are right to nurture your earth and also support them with the changes in your frequency, for the actions alone will make no difference. It is the increase in the *frequency of compassion plus action that creates change.*

When there is only the focus upon the money or the political position to make changes in how you are living on your planet then there is no connection to the true purpose of changing the way you treat the earth. You would not do the things you do if you knew you were connected. It is like buying someone a gift but deep down you hate them...does the person not feel the true frequency of your action?

Your earth can still expand. You can still live in a space that supports you and that you are comfortable with, but you cannot continue to live in the disconnected way you are now and expect your earth to be supportive of that. It cannot.

You blame the industrial age...hmmm...but who created it and why was it created? It was a key time in your disconnection although it started even before then. This has been present for many centuries, in many different forms and it does not need to take that long to shift. We wish to also let you know that this was not a paid political announcement! Although as universal keepers we do have a deep interest in what is happening.

The power of one Being

Remember who you are, Young Ones, as you make your decisions about what to do with your life because it all starts with you making that decision to reconnect to your Expanded Being again. The power of what one Being can create is expansive.

The more you live from the space of the Expanded Being, the stronger will be your connection to the planet you live within and to the stars you are connected to. It is the time in which the relationship between all things is paramount. It is the time for this to come forward into each Being's awareness, it is time for you to expand beyond your earthly consciousness into a new realm of awareness, into a new era of connection for this is required for the continuation of humanity.

Your role is to rejuvenate your planet

There are many Beings existing on this planet whose purpose has always been to connect to their Expanded Being, to be this Energy for others to feel. Their roles may not be ones of the teacher, but their roles are ones in which their light, their frequency, is transferred to the very earth itself, to the very core, to its Being. For these Beings are required to rejuvenate this space that all people live within. The degeneration of the human Spirit continues and the energetic expression of separation is spreading and the Quickening we have spoken of is in response to this.

There is a critical mass, there is a time that is nearing in which a call to the Expanded Being is required. It is the time for those of you who are Beings of the expansive Energy of compassion to spread a new Energy across your community, it is you remembering who you are, who you have been and accepting this space again.

The planet is feeling an urge to shift, there is a sense that the planet itself is in turmoil, that the earth is reflecting its fury back to its inhabitants because of how it is being treated and the way you treat each other. There is an opening, a crack in the field in which a new light is wishing to spread across this land, and there are those who need to thrust their hands into the crack to allow their own light to expand the brilliance of this.

The crack, as we are calling it, is a new emergence of Energy, a new wave of change that will be powered and generated by those who are deciding to take the next step. The Energies of the planet are indeed in need of a new shift, the consciousness of those who are ready have been calling to us in a unified voice through the shared frequency of compassion. That is why we, and others, are here. That is why you are here.

Chapter 11

Family & Relationships

You have been born into many families, you have experienced many different expressions of Self within those families in many different forms as a physical Being at different times in your own history. You have also experienced many different relationships throughout each existence, and all these aspects have gone into making up who you currently are.

When you understand your connection to your family and to your partners, you will see a much bigger picture of the role all relationships play in your existence and this will bring you great freedom and release from those ties that you feel keep you stuck and in pain.

Your connection to your family

Let us begin our conversation with your siblings, your sisters and your brothers, so that you can understand how your connection to your family works. You are all born of the same stock, from the same parents so why is there such a difference between you? Many of you have been aware of these differences since you were small children playing together. Such different interests, different ways of responding in the games you played and yet you were all raised in the same house with the same rules and even the same parents...curious, is it not? Why do I argue with them so? They were born a few years after me...that must be why the difference is present. But even when they were born you could see the difference, could you not? And also there are great similarities present, so how can this be?

Each of you is a combination of Energies. As we have spoken with you already, there are the frequencies that you bring with you from all of your previous existences that make up your Energetic expression of Self, and then there are the frequencies of the family and your environment that you have chosen and that you respond to.

The aspects of you that are the same as your siblings are the same because you are part of a family unit that you have all chosen. That family has a particular frequency, a particular Energy that is a part of each of its members and part of the field that surrounds it and this is what creates the connection between you all. And you are also different because you have each had your own unique experiences in previous existences, you have each had your own learning and growth as well as areas where you have held yourself back from expanding into your connection with your Expanded Being. So you also have your own unique frequency which is different to the others in your family, and this is expressed through your personality, your interests and your physical form.

Many of you feel so connected to your family and there is a good reason to be connected, for they are part of your learning, they play a role in you understanding so much about yourself in this existence. You have chosen them because they also create a space in which you can choose to grow beyond the limitations that you feel your family imposes upon you.

Your family is a frequency match

You choose your family in each existence because of the frequency of that group. You choose them based on your past existences, based on what you have understood and not understood and what you are choosing to learn and release in this existence. You do not choose them based on the identities of the Beings within that family. When you are back with us between your existences, you choose to be born into a family frequency that will give you the opportunity to create the changes you wish for.

It has been misunderstood that you go through many lifetimes with the same Beings, that you were once the mother, the brother and the lover of the same person. This is not the way it happens, for you are not working things out in your existence through the identity or human personality of another Being. You do not follow a person, as you call them, through many existences so that you can be many different expressions towards them. Energetically you will see similarities and connections with your family and in your relationships, but they exist at the Energetic level and not at the level of the individual. It is because you all connect so deeply to the limited expression of your physical identity that you assume you must move through time together because of your closeness in this existence.

This would get very complicated and messy in our filing system when you think of all the relationships you have, and all the relationships those people have with others who you may not have a deep connection with! And if this were to be so, you would limit your learning in each existence because you would always be with the same Beings. The universe is not set up in this way, Young Ones, because All That Is wants you to all expand and grow into the fullest expressions of your Being so that the universe itself may expand.

Unfinished business

So you choose your family based on the match of your

frequency and theirs not because of the individuals that exist within it. When you see it in the form of layers of existence, of frequencies of expression rather than individual Energies being reunited, you will understand that you choose your parents because their Energy resonates with where you are as you *begin* in the existence, not because you had a previous existence with them or because there is unfinished business to be resolved.

The only unfinished business you have to resolve, if you wish to think of it in that way, is with your own Self. It is never with anyone else. So there are no karmic contracts, or soul agreements that you have made that you need to work out in this or any other existence with anyone except your own essence.

And we know for many of you there is a very strong emotional connection to some members of your family. It may be a parent, a grandchild, a sibling and you feel that you are more closely connected to them than to others and so you have assumed it is because you have a past life connection with them. The differences in connection and emotion that you feel with some people is real, but it is because of your resonance and connection in this existence, it is because of the connection your Being feels with their Being. So you see, you are experiencing a much deeper connection than one purely due to a shared history, as so many believe.

This connection Being to Being is your goal, for when you are feeling this you are experiencing the sameness of another, you are feeling the compassionate Energy of their essence and you resonate so closely with it because it is the same as yours. It is a much deeper connection than anything you have understood before, and it is an experience to be celebrated for it shows the depth of your connection to your Expanded Being.

Take a moment now, Young Ones, to turn to the back of the

book and explore the **Practice of Understanding the Family Frequency** that we have brought forward for you. Use this as an opportunity to feel what it is we are saying, to gain your own understanding of your true connection to your family.

Your journey is unique to you

We can hear your thoughts as you read these words, and even your arguments! We see that many of you are very attached to the idea of travelling through many existences with another Being, perhaps a soulmate whom you cannot bear to be parted from, or a much-loved parent who has shown you such caring in this existence and you are saddened at the thought of not being with them in your next.

Take a moment to reflect on this, Young Ones, to reflect on the individual journey each Soul is undertaking. The key here is that your journey is unique to you, the speed at which you expand, the depth to which you reconnect to your Expanded Being in each existence is a choice only you can make. Many of you make great movement forward in an existence, releasing many of the limitations and restrictions of Self that held you back in your previous lives and there are those of you who do not. It is always your choice.

If you do make these changes, your frequency will change. Then in your next existence you will choose a family, relationships and a place to exist based on *that* frequency. The final choice is not known until you are here with us planning your next adventure. Let us paint a picture of this for you, so you can understand the implications of this new understanding.

Imagine that you have found your soulmate in this existence, and that you love them so dearly that you are sure you have had previous lives together and that you will travel through time together in your future existences as well. With this depth of connection, let us assume that you both have a very similar frequency, that Energetically you are much alike.

Now let us imagine that in this existence, your soulmate hears the calling of their Being to expand even further, to live in the full expression of their Being, to know that they are the creative Energy of All That Is and that they truly are a spiritual Being enjoying experiences on the physical plane. This is not just something they are thinking would be nice to experience, it is an expression at the level of their Being and so their frequency will shift to reflect this, will it not?

Now let us imagine that, for whatever reason in this existence, you do not hear the urgings of your Being as clearly, that although it is something you are open to it is not something you feel as strongly. It is not something you embody at the level of your Being. So while your frequency may grow in this existence due to your experiences and understandings, it does not expand to the same extent as your soulmate's does. The frequency of your Beings continues to be shaped by your individual experiences and choices in your life together, and you grow old and eventually leave your physical expressions of Self behind and return to All That Is to plan your next existence.

When you are back here with us, it is clear that your frequencies are now quite different and so the next existence you each choose will be different. You will select different families to match your frequency, perhaps even a different country and the timing for your return will also be particular to you. You make all of these choices because your Beings have one purpose that guides them and that is to continue their own expansion and to continue contributing to the Energetic shifts on your planet and in the universe.

So can you see, Young Ones, why your Beings will not *physically* be together in your next life, for you would never choose to hold another Being back on their journey of expansion just so you could have them with you. And here is the piece that many of you may not have recognised, but it is the one that will give you great comfort while you are so identified with your physical form, and that is the fact that while you may not physically journey forward together your Beings are always connected for how can it be otherwise when you are all part of the connected Energy of All That Is?

You are your own soulmate

This fear of loss or separation is an expression of the Constricted Self and it only exists when you identify so strongly with your physical forms. All of this information is offered to you so that you can expand beyond that sense of Self and recognise your true expansive natures. The example we have given you is the most common that you will experience through your existences. And it can also happen that you share more than one existence with a Being, but the misunderstanding that this is how it will *always* be will indeed hold you back.

So grow together if you wish and allow the space to unfold compassionately, never holding on too tight or holding the other back, but always allow your journeys to become the fullest expression of your Expanded Beings to unfold.

Can you see, Young Ones, how the search for a soulmate can only come from a space where you do not feel whole yourself? Many of you feel that a soulmate will complete you, but how can *they* complete you when you are the only one who can do that for yourself? When you know yourself to be the same Energy as All That Is and that there is no separation between any Energies, then you will come to the recognition that you are all soulmates, for you are really all aspects of the same divine Soul of creation.

You resonate deeply with a soulmate, as you call them, because they may reflect what it is you need to do or become to connect more fully with your Expanded Being. When you feel that energy so strongly, it can sometimes be misinterpreted as love and then if the relationship falters, you sink deeper into the abyss and identify more strongly with your Constricted Self and your feelings of unworthiness or pain.

You are all worthy of love for you *are* love, you *are* the frequency of compassion, you simply need to know and to feel this to be your true expression. You may have many soulmates in your lifetimes and they are all there as part of your growth.

Understanding your family lineage

Now let us go back to your family, for there is a further understanding to be had in this realm of your existence as well. Let us look at your family tree and all the lines of connection you can see upon the page. You look at it and say, This is me, this is who I am. These are my ancestors and their history has shaped who I am today. But this is not you, for this is only a page about flesh and it has no reference to energy at all.

Your family members are not connected to you through deep lineage over many generations, they are connected to you through a shared frequency that you have chosen to connect with in this existence. There will be similarities because of the frequency, but there will also be great differences because of their experiences and because you are unique Beings.

So we hear you ask, But what does this mean about my family tree, DZAR, what about the sense of connection and place I have because of that, because of my family history? Can you feel, Young Ones, how deep your desire for connection is when you say this? How deeply you desire this sense of belonging to a group that is much larger than the one you see around you in your immediate family? It is a deep calling for many of you, is it not?

Take a moment to feel where that deep expression and desire comes from, sit quietly and feel its expression. Some of you can feel that there are two aspects to it and some of you will have awareness of just one of them. Let us look at these two aspects now.

The two feelings many of you will be aware of come from different aspects of Self which are expressing this desire for connection. At its deepest level, this desire is coming from your Expanded Being which is always seeking to move from any sense of separation back to the experience of connection with all other Beings and with All That Is.

It is this desire which generates the feelings of love and compassion you express to those you call your family, it is this desire that calls you forward to create a connection to those in your family who may be dispersed across your globe.

At the next level, the desire to be a part of a family lineage that you can trace on paper is coming from the Constricted Self which feels incomplete on its own. So it seeks to attach itself to ancestors who perhaps had standing in your community or who did brave and noble deeds so that it can feel larger and more whole. Very often when the connection to a family heritage is made from this expression of Self, it serves only to further restrict the Being for it becomes so emotionally identified with its physical family that it can further deepen its sense of difference and separation from others.

At its most extreme, this is where racial prejudices and family feuds that last for generations come from, the sense that because you did a harm to one of my forbears then I have a responsibility to right that wrong, to avenge them. Can you not see how this serves only to create even more separation on your planet? It moves you further from your goal of compassionate connection with *all* Beings, because your focus is constricted to those who share your family name or bloodline.

The role of your family

There are many aspects for you to understand when you are born into a family unit for that is why you have chosen it. And we have heard many of you wonder why you would have chosen the family experiences you have, for you do not think of them as joy-filled or loving. So we wish to explore this now with using Mary and Gary's lives to give you understanding on this point. Is it not lucky that they provide such helpful examples for our teachings? You may be wondering if it is simply a coincidence that their lives are useful in this way or if it is part of something larger that we planned long before they were aware of their connection with us...and we would say, there are no coincidences!

Every Being is different because of the experiences you have allowed to become you. And so, there are different things, different experiences that you choose to be a part of in order to release, to learn and to grow in each existence. The family unit that you choose when you are here with us, is chosen to allow you to do just this.

So let us introduce Mary and Gary into this story, for they both came into this existence looking for the same thing, they came looking to experience connection. One chose and grew up in a family in which connection was present and the other chose a family in which connection was not a part of the experiences growing up. Looking from the level of your physical reality, many of you would see two completely different families and childhood experiences and you may label some of them good or bad, happy or otherwise.

So while their end points were the same, each of them chose a very different family frequency based upon their experiences from previous existences. So do you not find it interesting that while their paths have varied greatly in the experiences accepted or not, they are both at a space in time now when they are joined on the same path? They have both come to a time in this current existence, where their life, their expressions of Self are all about connection, it is all about how to be connected and how to *be* the connection itself.

There are many ways in which you can incarnate to become a fuller expression of your Expanded Being. Some of you have decided to enter a family in which hardship is present or you may have chosen a loving family to become your fullest expression. They are different paths, all with the same destination and you will continue to experience different paths until you realise what your true destination is.

So who then is to say that one family is good and the other not? For the family serves its purpose based on the expression of Self you bring into your existence and the outcome you have decided upon, and *you* have chosen it all.

As your awareness of your connection to your Expanded Being becomes stronger, you will choose families in your future existences that will reflect your knowing because that is how you evolve, you evolve through knowing. And the more you know who you are, the simpler and more joy-filled each incarnation becomes.

So Young Ones, the more you can release the labels and judgements many of you have placed upon the experiences of your family, the faster you will see the path in front of you where you will experience more joy and more compassion in your existence. And your family in this existence will either be on the path with you, or not. If they join you, then welcome them. Welcome them from the true sense of your compassionate Being without the judgements of the past to haunt you. If they do not, then allow them to be, as they are on the same journey as you but it is *their* journey. Show them the compassion of who *you* know yourself to be and most of all release your attachment to your experiences so that you can release yourself.

You are not linked to your family's past

Physically there are no links to your family's past for you are only a part of this family now. Can you see how liberating this is for you? Can you feel how much easier it is for you to release any limited expressions of Self that you have experienced due to your family's history of poverty, physical illnesses or persecution when you understand that you are not weighed down by the burden of generations of repeated experiences of limitation?

Your family is the frequency of the expressions that you have chosen to learn and release in *this existence*. Each family member has an aspect in common, you all have awarenesses to learn from the family group, it is why you have all chosen to be a part of that Energetic form. Although there is a very high probability that you have never existed together as a unit. There may have been a connection in previous existences with some of them, but you do not have the Beings of the one family following each other around from existence to existence for as we have explained that would slow down your expansion very quickly.

You do not stalk each other across time...we think there are universal laws against stalking! I tried to shake that Energy in the last life and here they are again! Do not fear, Young Ones, it does not work in that way.

The confusion comes because you are all trying to understand this from a linear concept, from the physical form trying to make sense of an Energetic existence. Your minds are truly not equipped to understand all the intricacies of the Energy that you are, and of course you are doing your best to make sense of this with what you have available. That is how you have always done it and your minds and your physical brains are expanding in their capacity to become aware of more.

Soon the time will come where you will all have the ability to transcend the bondage called your mind that you have placed around your ability to be aware. When that moment comes, you will sit back and laugh at what you used to think was true for you will have expanded your physical mind and your spiritual form and released the separation between them both.

Chapter 12

Time &
The Space of Becoming

Time is inherent in everything you do, inherent in all of your experiences. There are many who have said that time is a construct, something that has been created for Beings to work within, meaning that time does not exist, that there is space in which everything just is. And so there is. The two planes coexist in the same moment, the two planes talk to each other, reflect each other and you may move between them both, but understand this, the plane you live within has time as a component.

For you to exist functionally within the physical plane you call earth, you must exist within its time, so it is helpful for you to understand how time really works.

You are Time Lords

If indeed time is a construct, it is reflective of the society you live within, it is reflective of the Being within that time for it is you who construct it. Think now of the city you live within, recognise how time moves within that place. For many it seems so fast, so chaotic that there is never enough time. Then there is the space where you leave your normal environment, you stop your daily activities and you rest. Many of you travel to a different culture where the sense is that time slows. But time is constant; it does not shift in how long it takes for a second to occur, so the only thing that is changing is you. Yet so often you blame time because it is too slow, it is too fast, your life is so short. But everything is reflective of the Being experiencing it, time is reflective of *who* you are, your experience of time reflects your expression of Self in each moment.

So you are indeed Time Lords for you have the ability to bend time, to play with time. You can make time into a form that works for you rather than making time work against you, as many of you do and then you blame it, you curse it. This is an important piece to understand in your growth, for is it not interesting that something that is so constant, that you factually know is fixed in its movement, can also be so flexible based on who you are in the moment?

Many of you also think that *you* are also fixed, that you are unable to truly change because of your past experiences, because of your environment, because of our family, your physical expression. And if this is what you think, can you see why you so often miss the changes that are presented to you, the changes that *are* occurring in each moment? How often do you look upon pictures of yourself when you were young and notice how much you have changed? Do you remember the things you used to believe so strongly to be true when you were younger, but now with your expanded knowledge you dismiss them as the follies of youth and you laugh at how you could ever have thought such things.

Throughout your existence you change physically and mentally of course, and you also change Energetically but because of your perception of time and your perception of Self you do not recognise the changes. Your view of time as you begin to age also shifts. Whilst growing up, as you say, time can seem so slow and then as you become older your perception is time goes so quickly. Can you begin to see the pattern? It is all you, it always has been. So the piece for you to accept and to be aware of is who you are in each moment, what is your expression of Self, for it is the sense of Self in that space of time that creates how time is perceived.

Your expression of Self creates time

So in order to shift and make time work for you, you must indeed shift the Self. You must become aware of the expression of the Being that is perceiving the time for that is the only way you can shift it and you do this already, Young Ones. Consider the times where you have indeed changed time by shifting the state of the Being perceiving it. When you are caught in the moment, when the awareness of Self and your experience are one and there is no separation between them you say that time flies. And then there are the times when you perceive it as separate from you, when you feel that a situation is shaping you, restricting you in your movement, so you judge the experience and therefore the Self perceives time to drag, to linger, to endure.

As you are reading these pages, become aware of the expression of Self that is present. How many pages do you read? Does time disappear when the Self is engrossed? Does time tend to get in the way when the words seem to fit uncomfortably with you, when you disagree with what is being said? These are important pieces, for you will begin to understand how you indeed manipulate your own time, how you interact with the field of Energy that surrounds you. You manifest your experience of time from the expression of Self that perceives it. All of these go forward into making time reflect in a way that either works or does not work for you in that moment.

As you continue upon your journey and become more connected to your Expanded Being, you will learn how you can indeed become the master of time, for you will begin to understand how to be in the space where time does not exist. From this space, you still can be a part of time and function within your current world, for it will not serve you to function above it, you have chosen this place so you can work within it. Upon working within it, you can begin to change how it is indeed formed and then create more space and time for every Being that exists within it. It all begins with you and the time is now, perfect timing!

Have compassion for your own Being

We know you have the understanding that there are other lives you have existed within, so we do wonder why you take this one so seriously! You become so impatient with your progress, you become angry with your growth. Let us look at your journey upon a scale of when you first came to this plane, your very first existence, to where you are now and how many other existences it will take until you finally leave.

You currently view this one existence from your point of entering to your point of leaving, and this becomes the whole focus of who you are. You look at your life and say, I am no longer a young person, why am I not enlightened, why isn't my spiritual journey complete, I've been working at it for many years! And on this plane you may, in fact, be rather old compared to others, but you may still be a young Soul along your spiritual path. For while you may have had many existences you are still young to us! If you saw such a young Soul, a young child struggling to understand its place in the world, would you chastise it for being so slow to learn? No, you would offer your wisdom to this young one to aid its development, to give it understanding. That is why we are here, to aid you with your development, to give you understanding and encouragement as a Being that still has many lives left to live.

The meaning of this is again all about compassion for Self.

Just as you would be compassionate to the young child who was learning, you also need to be compassionate with yourself. In this existence you may feel struggle, you may feel overwhelm and so many of you judge yourself harshly because of what you have done or not done, for the mistakes you have made. But what do these judgements do? Do they help you to learn and to grow, or do they restrict you, do they make you feel small? You think you should know better because of the age you are, but can you see how time can deal you a fickle blow? How old are you really in the big scheme of your existences, in the eternal life of your Being? Can you begin to see, Young Ones, what we are wishing to say to you?

It is not the time for you to be argumentative towards yourself, it is not the place for you to be harsh to your young form as you seek to understand who you are in this world. It is the time for you to take a bigger understanding, a more compassionate look at your growth, no matter what your age is now in this existence. Your age now is not important; what is important is that you are on the road to accepting your eternal Soul and its expansion, you are in the space of becoming all that you can be, of becoming the fullest expression of who you truly are.

Allow this awareness to relieve the pressure, for this is about you allowing yourself the space to be compassionate to yourself again. That is why we offer this story to you, that is why we wish you to understand more about time so that you can look at it from many different angles, to be aware of how it affects you now, to understand the development that you have been through in your past, and to have awareness of your true age, the true age of your Being.

Your future is already here

It has been said that time is not a linear thing, it is not something that can be viewed from a past to a present to a future, yet it is how many of you understand it. And if that is the understanding that is needed for you to be able to accept a bigger picture then so shall it be. For as you begin to accept this, you will begin to see more, you will begin to see how your past is reflected already in the now, how your now is projecting the future that is already present with you.

You will begin to see so much more when you allow the constraints of how you view time to be released, but first view it from what you know. Open your eyes to the greater expanse of who you have been and who you are becoming. Your future is already here, it is already accessible to you, it just needs the openness of the mind to be able to accept it. It needs the compassion of the Being to be open, to lead the way, to guide you through the avenue of you.

So when you next look at your watch...what will the time say then, how will you view the hands upon its face? They are saying so much more to you than just the time, are they not? The space for you to awaken, the time for you to reconnect is all perfect, it is all now.

The space of becoming

When you decide, when you begin on your journey of reconnection to your Expanded Being and to the Energy of All That Is, the one thing we wish you to release is how long it will take to get to where you think you should be going. For when you do, you will understand that the need for suffering along a path of joy and compassion is not required. There may indeed be times when an aspect of pain is present but you will know why, you will be able to alter the expression of Self that is manifesting the pain, learn its lessons and then let it go. For understand, as you are connecting to your Expanded Being you are coming in sync with the universal frequency of compassion, and compassion is not struggle, compassion is not you having to give up anything.

In this space of becoming, you decide to release whatever is not the fullest expression of your Expanded Being. What a joyous time this is, Young Ones, for these Energies that have become a part of you from previous existences are also wishing to return home to All That Is, their job is at an end, their time with you is also at an end. They are wishing to come back, to be released into the expanding compassionate field of All That Is.

So when you release an aspect of Self which you feel is not your true expression, you are releasing an Energy that will expand the universal field of compassion. By you becoming more, you allow the universe itself to expand; by you allowing your burden to lift, the stars will begin to shine brighter this night. For everything has its purpose, everything has a meaning. It is all Energy, it is all expression and it will re-join the larger field of compassion as do you as you move along your journey of becoming. Can you feel the cycle? Can you begin to see how the system works? There is no longer a point to you holding on for you do not need to hang on to what has restricted you. By you becoming more, by you releasing what has held you back, you become a part of expansion itself, you become a part of the compassionate expression of this universe.

Imagine the planet that you exist within now as more and more people do this...can you sense how the Energy will shift around you? Can you sense how your connection to the other will grow, that your sense of separation and separateness will disappear? If you looked upon the person next to you with as much love as you look upon your own child, what would the world be like then?

Your journey of becoming is such a joyous one, Young Ones, that when you are living from this space of connection and compassion you will not want to miss a step along your path. There is no hurry, there is no judgement of the time your changes are taking, for your Expanded Being exists in each moment connected to the expansive Energy of All That Is and in that space all is exactly as it should be.

Celebrate each step along your path

If you have young children, would you even consider jumping straight to their 21st birthday and missing all the years of their growth, the celebrations of the milestones and the joy of watching them grow up? Of course not, and yet you wish to do this with yourself. We do not wish you to miss the journey, for it is one that is filled with so many milestones and celebrations, that if you could see what we can, you would not even think of skipping ahead!

The space of becoming is the experience of the Expanded Being with its awareness and its acceptance of the role time plays in your expansion. Then there is the other space, the one of the Constricted Self, the one that is not full, the one that feels its emptiness, the one that is constantly in a hurry, it seeks pleasure to relieve its pain, it wishes experience to manifest instantly. How many of you have seen the thing that you wish for materialise instantly before your eyes and yet you still feel hollow after it is consumed? Is it not familiar? Emptiness can lead to more emptiness. If you look for the quick fix, if you ask the universe to manifest something to fill the void that exists around you, then all you will receive in return is more emptiness, for that false sense of abundance will not fill you, that instant gratification will last but a glimpse.

For look at what is occurring, Young Ones, what is the expression of the Being asking for this immediate gratification? Where is the depth and acceptance in the understanding that you are in the space of becoming your fullest expression of Self and that as you are shifting and expanding it can take your world around you time to do the same?

The universe is truly abundant and compassionate and it feels the emptiness of the Constricted Self that lies beneath the request. As we have said earlier, there is nothing wrong with you having what you wish in this life, for in fact that is what we want for you also but the universe will only resonate with the Being that is asking from the space of connection to its essence and it will respond only to that frequency.

When you ask from your Expanded Being, you feel complete and there is no hole to fill. So if you wish to experience an aspect of life filled with abundance in any form, then begin by being the Being that is reflective of this space, of this reality. The experience of an

Expanded Being will not be altered if it is surrounded by treasure or surrounded by sand, because the inner peace, the inner joy, is always its expression and it does not need these things to be happy, for it is happy now.

And we understand that many of you may feel that this space of acceptance and wholeness is unattainable, and it *is* unattainable if you think that you can jump from where you are now to there, to move in a single leap to the complete expression of expansion and abundance. But if you begin your journey with the decision that every day you will allow more of this expression in, that you will choose to *be* more of this expression as often as you can, then you may also be surprised at how quickly your changes manifest, you may be delighted at what falls at your feet. When you do this, you will begin to see a benevolent universe, you will begin to feel that someone is listening, that you are connected, and that you are not alone.

So be compassionate with yourself, Young Ones, and with the time it takes for your journey. Enjoy the experience along the way, for we can tell you that it will not all be completed in a single existence for any of you! You will celebrate your journey throughout many existences, until you become the complete expression of your Expanded Being living on this physical plane and then it will be time for you return here to us. Your journey on earth will be complete and you will be ready to choose another form of existence and to experience and continue your expansion in a new realm.

Chapter 13

How To Manifest
From The Space Of Your Being

We have seen so many of you wishing for something that you do not have, something to fill a part of your room, your house, your garage, an aspect of Self that you feel is missing. You ask for it sincerely from a deep place within you and nothing arrives upon your doorstep. Nothing seems to change in your experiences and then you raise your fists towards the heavens and you curse because we do not listen. Yet time and again, the expression of Self that is doing the asking is the key factor to you receiving what you ask for.

The universe listens to the frequency of your Being

You are Beings of Energy and so the words you speak, the thoughts you think and the Self are all vibration and they send their frequencies into the Energetic field that surrounds you. You have all had times when you have said a word or shown a feeling, yet the true thought or feeling behind it is different to what you have displayed. Two vibrations go out, but one will be stronger than the other and you can guess which one it is.

The same thing happens when you are asking for something. The request has a frequency, but the vibration of the Constricted Self that has the frequency of insecurity or lack which is behind it is stronger than the asking. Many times you ask for big things, big events, big changes to fill these insecurities but nothing is as big as that insecurity that is asking. That is why so many times you do not receive what you ask for.

As the universal Energy hears what it is that you wish, it hears it from the true space of who you are in the asking, from the space of your Expanded Being and it will send down that which it hears. Yet many of you miss so much of what is sent to you, for although you may be in the space of your Expanded Being when you ask, you then move out of that space into the doubt, into the limitation of the Constricted Self as you are waiting for the manifestation to occur. In this space, you do not have awareness of what is possible and waiting for you. You miss out on all the ways in which it is presented to you because you become so focused on your old expression of Self, you become so focused on the space of *how and when* you think it should manifest.

We wish you could see the Returns Desk for unclaimed requests at All That Is! It is so vast that we have many Energies working 24/7 putting the returned desires that people miss back on the shelves. Your name is still on it, it is still there waiting for you to be ready to accept it, but many of them have dust upon them for they have been there through many of your existences. Our wish is to be able to close the Returns Desk, our wish is for you to receive all of the things that you ask for that are in alignment with you living as the fullest expression of your essence, for why would an abundant universe wish for anything else?

Who you are in the asking

There are many components that go forward to allowing manifestation to occur in your life. The first is always the expression of Self that is asking for what it is you are wishing. Are you looking at the things you want through Expanded Eyes, are you asking from the space of your Expanded Being or from a connection to your Constricted Self?

Many times your requests come from the Constricted Self, from the space of lack. And you have noticed, have you not, that when you ask from that space that you are still unhappy a short time after even when you receive your wish for, it has not filled the hole. And there is the time when nothing arrived and that reflected upon the emptiness inside you and it felt at that time that it indeed made the hole bigger within you. You decided that the universe does not listen to you and you separated yourself even further from your Expanded Being and from us.

Can you feel, Young Ones, the many times you have tried to make something happen but it just added to your own doubt, to your own fears? At these times, you were left with the sense of I knew it wouldn't work! I never get what I want. Understand the Self that is saying these things, understand that you are saying these things to yourself from the space of your Constricted Self for your Expanded Being would never have such a conversation with you. Can you begin to see how then the experiences become you?

When you are identified with your Constricted Self, you begin with much good will and intent for you expanding. But then if it does not work the way you wish, you place so much doubt within your own field that your expression of Self becomes even more limited and feels even more separate. You allow the emptiness and the disappointment to *become* you.

So each time you sit quietly and connect to your Expanded Being, to that aspect of you that is connected to the Energy of All That Is and to the Energy of creation, *know* that if your request is truly coming as an expression of your true essence that it is *always* answered. Each time you ask from this space, know that you have successfully completed the task you have set yourself to do. Then all there is for you to do is to stay connected to your Expanded Being and have awareness of what unfolds around you. It is resonance, it is how the universe functions. It will not deny you but so many times you feel that you are denied and that experience becomes attached to your expression of Self and your pain deepens.

Know this too, that if you ask for something that you want from the space of your Constricted Self, if you are asking because you believe the thing you want is the key to you feeling whole, to you feeling happy, that it will make you feel worthy then it is very unlikely, Young Ones, that you will experience what it is you seek. For again it all comes back to the expression of Self that is doing the asking.

You cannot *pretend* to be the expression of your Expanded Being, it is not something you can lay over the top of your Constricted Self to try to dress it up in your eyes or ours for we always respond to the true frequency of your request. We are not fooled by the fancy packaging it may come in! But when you ask from the space of your Expanded Being, you are in the space of becoming the true expression of your essence and so you make your request for the sheer joy of the experiencing who you are in that space. When you know that you are complete without it, and yet you seek the experience for your own growth and joy, that is when we really listen to you!

Awareness and acceptance return again as the way for you to move out of the space of the Constricted Self. Acceptance that a whole Being lives within you already, and awareness from the space of your wholeness of what is being delivered to you in that moment and, indeed, in the moments preceding it. Understand, Young Ones, this is a practice, understand that you are in the space of becoming more strongly connected to your Expanded Being and the more you connect, the stronger your awareness, and the more joy you will experience in your existence.

Giving All That Is a delivery deadline

Awareness and acceptance come back again and again. These two words have great depth and they are what allow you to see what is being given, it is where time may work against you again, because of the reflection of who you are. You set a deadline, you expect these things to happen within an instant, a week, a month and when that time is up you say, Damn universe, never listens to me!

As we have discussed already, time is a reflection of you. You set an arbitrary time that works against you, the two of you are in cahoots; your limited Self and your view of time working to keep the status quo, working to keep you stuck in your Constricted Self. One thing we can say for sure as you move along the path, much will be shown, much will be given and it will all be due to the direct reflection of who you are in each moment.

So if you are not receiving what it is you wish in the time frame you allowed it to be present, then what do you need to do? Look inward, look at the expression of Self that is doing the asking *and* the expression of Self that is doing the waiting! For they will both be part of the Energetic field you are creating that is either allowing your changes and requests to manifest or they will be holding them at bay.

The abundance of the Self comes first

So always begin by looking inwards, Young Ones and we hear you say, Again! I grow weary of looking inwards, at having to change myself I just want it to happen now...

We also grow weary of seeing you struggle, for we have watched you for many lifetimes and we know you are so much more. We want you to know that we listen, to know that we hear what you ask and we will send what is required for you to move forward for that is abundance itself. The more you *become* the expression of your Expanded Being, the more possibility lies before you. Abundance is not only designed to fill your Christmas stocking, it is designed to fill your Soul and your heart for this is true abundance and it is where it must begin.

Do not be confused and limit abundance to a mountain of money, or a book of houses that you own. Many is the Soul that possesses all this and is still empty. But know that you can also be the fullest expression of your Expanded Being *and* have all of these things if you still want them, but it is the abundance of the Self that must come first.

So if the timing of what you are asking for is not working for you, then look within yourself, adjust your space, adjust who you are *being* in the asking and the waiting and then allow yourself to be open. Keep your eyes focused upon the sky, for many and anything could fall from it at your feet, wishing for you to bend down and pick it up instead of walking right over the top of it as you have done many times before.

How to ask from your Expanded Being

This is one of the most important keys to your expanding. This is where your awareness must begin its expansion because from the space you are now as your Constricted Self, your perceptions will indeed colour what you are expecting, what you think you'll see and feel. But when you ask from the space of the Expanded Being which is directly connected to the Energy of All That Is, you feel in the moment when you make the request that space within you of deep love for yourself. There is no doubt, there is no fear, there is simply the experience of your true essence.

That is all you need to do, Young Ones. You ask from the space of your Expanded Being and then you simply feel and connect deeply with the space within you that is the direct connection to All That Is and continue to focus upon that space. Be still and become aware of what is occurring in that moment. You do not need to focus upon what you have asked for, all you need to do is to focus upon the Self that is asking.

When you ask in this way, you allow two things to happen. Firstly, you allow you a deeper connection to who you are to be present. You feel and remember this space of your true essence again and you reconnect to this space within you. Secondly, you begin to open up a frameless picture for yourself, for you will begin to see and feel so much more of what is being presented to you without the cloud of perception of how it should be, of what must occur. From this space, you will hear the guidance of your Soul that will direct you to whatever actions will support the manifestation that you have initiated Energetically.

So we can say to you that if you do these two things, you will begin to recognise and to know that the universe is listening and that you are connecting to who you truly are.

You are all in the space of becoming your Expanded Being, so we know that many times the frequency of your requests may still be tinged with the Energy of your Constricted Self. We know that there are times when you are in such a space of darkness that you cannot even find the strength or the clarity to make the request that will lead you back to the light, back to your *in*-lightenment.

Take heart, Young Ones, because the universe can also hear what it is that you do not say, what it is that you do not vibrate. For remember that All That Is knows who you truly are, it knows where you are along your path and it knows when you are truly wishing to walk along the path and return home. When it feels your true frequency, even though you cannot, in its compassion and in its love for you it will support you even when you cannot ask for help yourself.

It is in these spaces when you feel most separate and disconnected from the compassion of the universe, that awareness is a key. For you may not get everything that you ask for but you *will* receive something, something small perhaps that will let you know that there is movement, that we are listening.

So expand your awareness, Young Ones, because so many times you miss what has been sent, you miss the message from us that we hear you and that we wish to support your journey. Take the steps along your journey home and the more steps you take, the more support you will feel from us.

Chapter 14

Why There Is Suffering & Pain

There is one question that is so often asked by you of Spirit, for you wish to understand why there is so much suffering and pain on your planet. How can these experiences be present in the existences of so many, when the true frequency of the universe is compassion?

We, too, look in amazement at the atrocities that one Being can commit against another, we look at the injustices that are committed against your fellow human beings, at the pain you create in your own and each other's lives and we feel your suffering and your question. Pain and suffering exist, Young Ones, because you have chosen them as the reminders of how far you have strayed from your own light.

The high cost of separation

These experiences on your planet are not expressions that

are connected to a compassionate universe; they are the result of Beings who are separated from Source, of Beings who have not recognised who they truly are. It is the unfortunate expression of a society in which the inhabitants have no awareness of Self, in which they have no awareness of the beauty and the essential sameness of the Being that sits beside them.

This is how atrocities occur, and your life will be shaped and added to by those experiences depending on your own connection to your essence, on your own understanding of yourself as an Expanded Being.

For those of you who remember who you are and the role experience is meant to play in your expansion, when you witness the pain around you or experience the suffering in your own life, you allow it to become the catapult for your search for a larger meaning, for your connection to something greater than the pain. So you do whatever you can to understand and release it and to connect ever-more strongly with your Soul. But for those who cannot hear the call of their Being to reconnect, for those who are not ready to let go of their Constricted Self, they will be consumed by the experiences and they will take them on as their own and separate even further from their Expanded Being and the compassion of All That Is.

Pain can be present for you in many forms, and the path away from it is always for you to connect to the part of you where the pain does not exist, to the part of you where the true expression of Self lies. The more you do this, the less pain and suffering will be present in your own life and there will also be less suffering on your planet because you will also shift the collective frequency of all Beings by your own connection and your own expansion.

The Self is never wounded

Many of you say, DZAR this is easier said than done! And we would ask you if living *as the pain* for the rest of your existence is an easier choice. When you are connected to your pain, Young Ones, you do not experience the pain as something that is separate from you, you experience it *as you*. No matter how your pain has manifested or the form of the suffering that you have existed within, we want you to know that this pain is not you and that you *can* change and create a different experience for yourself. It all begins with you releasing this physical identity that you currently attach yourself to so strongly, by releasing the expression of the Constricted Self that has been sculpted by the experiences of pain and suffering in whatever form they have taken.

Your current physical form and your true spiritual form are both real, they both exist simultaneously and you are always at the choice point. The spiritual form, your Expanded Being, often seems harder to obtain because you are so familiar with the pain, that you wonder how any other experiences can exist. Look deeply now at the expression of Self that is doing the experiencing, have awareness of how you are thinking and what you are focusing on, start to notice who you communicate with on a daily basis, listen to what your friends and family are saying to you, listen to what you are saying to yourself. Do each of these things support your connection to your Expanded Being or do they reflect and keep you connected to your pain and your Constricted Self?

Can you begin to see how much of your life you are creating every day, purely by what you are focusing upon? And if it is you doing it, can you not choose to do something different, can you not choose to listen to the light within you? For as faint as it may be, you will sense the difference between the two, you will begin to feel the difference between the expressions of the Constricted Self and the resonance of your Expanded Being. This is your place to start; this is the place for your hope to begin again or indeed for it to blossom, perhaps for the first time in this existence.

Use the Meditation we have brought forward with this book, use the Practice of the Expanded Being from these pages and *become* your Expanded Being, for that is the key to your change.

When you see that you are the creator of your world, you no

longer allow the pains you have experienced to dictate who you are. When you *know* that you are the Energy of creation, you can begin to shift so that you can live in connection with the compassion and abundance of the universe. Allow the presence of time to continue its cycle, do not place a timeframe on yourself to change, just give yourself to the daily practice of feeling the light within you, of feeling the compassionate presence of your Expanded Being. It is there to support you, it is there to help you exist in the space of pure joy.

A daily practice of joy

So, commit to the daily practice of the Meditation and of connecting to your Expanded Being, choose to look for something joyous, for something small to place a smile upon your heart and you will begin to see and experience your world differently. When you do this, *you will change* for that is why you are here and you are not meant to always live a life of pain, a life of separation. We know that eventually you will all see your light; eventually you will hear your true voice and the messages from your Soul, for it is only a matter of time until this is your experience.

Who decides that the time is right? You do. You can decide to begin now or you can wait for the next few lives to pass you by and decide then, but it *will* happen. That space is certain for we know who you truly are, we see who you are becoming and we wish you to see it also.

Chapter 15

The End of our
First Conversation

So Young Ones, we are nearing the end of our first conversation in this form and we have begun exploring some of the many aspects of your existence. It has been a frequency conversation between us, for that is how we communicate with you, not just at the level of the words you are reading on the page but through the vibration of our connection.

It has been a conversation between Beings and Energies that are connected, that come from the same Source, for now you can feel that our Energies are one, can you not? As you have read these words, emotions and feelings and even memories have become present, some are familiar and some are not. As you have completed the exercises and the Meditation that accompany this conversation, you have felt your connection to your Expanded Being and experienced changes. For many of you *have* connected and expanded, and for some it may be for the first time in your physical memory that you have felt this space.

Do you know, Young Ones, what is exciting about this? It is exciting because we know it won't be the last time that you feel your connection to your Expanded Being, for once the connection is made its Energy will always wish to expand. So for all of you reading and feeling this space, it is a beginning, a beginning of an expansive possibility for your expression of Self and for the experiences you will have in this existence.

So we welcome you, we embrace you and we will be there for you when you call, when you ask for guidance as the many before you have also received.

Your journey forward

As you have been reading this book, you have gone through an expansion program designed for you by Spirit and we can feel that many of you are becoming more aware and more expansive. You are becoming aware of the ways you have kept yourselves stuck through many lifetimes by identifying with, and becoming attached to, your experiences rather than releasing them and expanding your connection to your Being and to the Energy of All That Is. With this new awareness, you are beginning to understand the Self more and to accept the role you play in the unfolding story of your universe.

Many of you are realising that there is more to be done as you joyfully accept that you are now in the space of becoming and that it is the perfect place for you to be! You are realising your sense of connection or separation from where you wish to be and who you wish to be. You are wishing to step even more fully into the space of connection with your Soul, to live your life as the fullest expression of the joy and compassion that is your true nature. And you have free will to choose to continue or not. For it is always your choice and we are always here waiting for you to take your first steps, so that we can support you and rejoice in your journey.

Tapping into Universal Wisdom

With this new level of awareness and acceptance, with your decision to connect more strongly to your own Expanded Being, you can then begin to tap into a field that previously may have been distant to you. From this expanded expression of Self, you can begin to feel the Energy of the future and decide whether it is worthy of your attention or not, you can decide if it is a future experience that you want to move towards or to leave alone.

From this new expression of Self, you can communicate with the Energy of others and gain wisdom and understanding from them without the use of speech but purely by the awareness of Energy that connects you both. From this new space of connection, you can hear the messages from your Soul as you connect with the wisdom and guidance of your Being. As you do, you will move through your life with so much more joy and fulfilment than you have ever imagined...and yet you have felt it deep within you, have you not?

What you are doing in each of these experiences is learning to channel energy that is connected to you through your Energetic field. You are channelling the wisdom of your Expanded Being, you are sharing in the wisdom of other Beings to support your movement forward. Channelling is you connecting to this field that surrounds you, and becoming aware of the environment that you cannot see but that you can feel. For most of you, channelling is not having a group of Energies such as we are talking through your Being, it is you having Energetic conversations that allow you to tap into your own wisdom and the wisdom of All That Is.

As you feel your true sense of Self resonate within you, you will create a stronger and stronger connection as you do the practices and the Meditation. There are those in this book and you will find more on the website (www.thepathofdzar.com) Mary and Gary have created for you.

The message from your Soul

Your space is ever-expanding because of who you are becoming and because of what you are accepting about your true essence as an Expanded Being. This is the message from your Soul, this is the space in which you realise that you create your joy, that you create your sense of connection, that you create your own experiences as well as contributing to the experiences shared by all other Beings on your planet.

So as you continue your journey, allow yourself to be guided by the Energy that you feel within you, feel yourself connected to the space of compassion that supports your expansion and then follow your path. For we shall be present to welcome you as we feel your presence appear. It has always been acceptance and awareness. How much of each you become is up to you.

We wish you to know and to feel our gratitude for all you are *being* to expand the compassion and connection between all Beings on your planet.

Go with love, Young Ones, and we look forward to our next frequency conversation and to feeling the expansion of your Being as you hear more clearly the messages from your Soul.

Chapter 16

Q&A with DZAR

This section of the book is an edited selection of answers DZAR has given to people attending The Path of DZAR workshops and talks. You can also listen to a selection of Q&A podcasts at our website.

You'll feel that the Energy of these exchanges is very relaxed and compassionate and, at times, quite humorous which is the space that is created on the DZAR events.

As you read these questions and DZAR's answers to them, read them as if you had asked them and allow your understanding and expansion to unfold.

Why are people so closed...

Q Why are people so closed when I talk to them about the changes I'm making in my life, I think they often think I'm a lunatic...

A We welcome your lunacy...better to be a loony than be the sane one denying that the sky is falling. It is a difficult path is it not? It is one you have experienced many times before, your expression is different but your sense of Self is the same. The most important thing for you to release is the need to show everyone else for here is how the expression will occur. The more that you begin to connect to that light within you, to that confident, expressive, magnificent space that exists as you, you become the quiet sage where you can shift softly and subtly through a crowd without anyone realising your physical presence but feeling that there is something there.

What you will leave is a trail...it is almost like a scent...not that of a skunk!...but a scent just as strong that others will follow and then they will come and they will ask you and you will not be looking for them. There is the magic moment because they feel who you are and they just want to be in that space. That is how the sense and the shift begin. There will be those who feel the light within you and it will trigger that same question within them so that they ask, How can I change? There must be more, I know this is not my true expression, I know my life is not meant to be this way. Why does it seem to be so difficult every single time...

So understand this, the more you let go of trying to change the world the more you will change it because of who you are. The more you can build up the compassion and the scented-ness within you, the quieter you will become, the more magnetic you will be and people will follow your scent...we will call you Chanel*...a much more

---

* Humorously referring to Chanel perfume.

attractive scent!

Over this weekend Expanded Being, some of you may feel the sound of your Expanded Being, you may hear it ring or sing to you. Listen for it. It also has a scent, it is will be very specific do not be surprised if it is a scent that sticks in your nose for some time. There is nothing wrong, you do not need to go and see a physician but understand that it is you...not needing a shower, no...but just you finally listening to that true expression of you. Your senses become alive because your whole Being has become alive. So begin to listen, begin to become aware. Can you understand what we say? (Yes) We understand that there will be a more convincing 'yes' over the course of the weekend. (Group laughter)

Am I just kidding myself ...

Q Am I just kidding myself about my belief that I should be doing healing work...I've stopped trusting myself to know what to do...

A So understand the way that you are indeed asking the question, from the sense of Self that is asking it. No wonder there is the expression of doubt, no wonder there is the un-surety. There is a part of you that has a sense of what it is you like to do, there is a sense that you would like to give of yourself to others. It is surely time that you begin to give of yourself to yourself for that is where you all must start. You cannot truly give to another if you yourself are not whole. But DZAR do we ever become whole? When we do become whole you whip us off the planet and we sit up there with you...what is the purpose of that? (Group laughing)

Can we say that there are levels of wholeness, that we need Beings to express their completeness upon this planet so that others can be awakened to hear their own. You are in this space of becoming, you are all here asking the same question from the same space because the words that are within you are all the same. You know that there is more to who you are, there is no separation in fact there is no separation between the billions of others that you co-habit this place with. Some listen some do not, some are ready some are not you are among a crowd who are.

The answer to your question again will come from you, you will know perfectly, exactly what it is you need to do once you can begin to connect with that sense of you within, to the true expression of Self.

So many wish to heal others because there is also an emptiness within, it is a way that they express themselves to create a larger sense of Self. There are so many who are present who do it this way. How effective could you be in helping or healing another when you are complete, when you know your expression of Self and you breathe and you be it every moment of your day. What sort of Energy can become present that can be given to another from that space? It is vast it will never deplete you, it will only enhance your own knowing of who you are and so you become more of an expanded Being, you attract more people to your light, you become the flame that becomes the attractor.

Struggle in my life...

Q I've done a lot of struggle in my life due to programming...when we accept ourselves and let go of the identity that has been programmed, will things change?

A The understanding of programming is such a fascinating one. You are programmed to be programmed, are you not? Do you see all your literature that is written...because of this then that...

You believe that all the expressions in your life have somehow programmed themselves into your flesh, that you are this mechanical robot, that you are a computer that is in a fixed space. And you are right to some extent, if you only see yourself as a singular Being living a fleshy existence. That is not you! It is the purpose of this space of becoming the Expanded Being for you are not a Being whose whole life is to experience pain and struggle, you are a Being whose role is to be the light and the joy that is the true expression of creation itself. For you to be able to do this you have to resonate at that frequency. A frequency can shift and change, it is not programmed it just is. When you move the dial further along the band you are no longer listening to the station you were before you are in a new spot are you not?

You see if you consider yourself as a fixed Being who has been programmed from birth because of my parents, because of my religion then you see how you build the shell for your existence, that you are limited in your movement, that you have no ability to break out of it. But that is not you! If you could remember how many existences you have been through and some of them, may we say, were a little shocking to watch you would be quite happy with where you are right now. (laughing) But again all those were not you either, they were experiences for that was your role for being here, you are not a fixed Being, you are not a stuck entity you are fluid, you are elegant.

It is about you reconnecting to that fluidity again regardless of the experience you had, it is not programmed it is there for you to hear, to learn and as soon as you learn it, it can be released. It can come back to us so it can be renewed and re-used as part of the compassionate universe. You see you have that role, you use the Energy and then you set it free...that is not programming! Can you understand? (Yes) So tell me who you are? Where is the flow? Let me hear (What I wanted to say was everything.)

That is what you wanted to say but you did not! That is the

piece for you. Do you see how you hold yourself back, how you keep yourself separate? You say it with your words but your expression is completely different. The you that you know yourself to be and the way you hold yourself back is the space for you to release.

What you have always done is hold yourself back, it was there so you could set yourself free and you do sometimes but then you run scurrying back to the cage, it's more comfortable there, nice hay to lay on...it's getting a little old. Can you feel this? (Yes) Yes you can, so that is what you are here to let go of? Will you? (Yes) Hmm...it's getting better, there's a bit more determination, we will watch. Wait until you shine...we don't want to wait too long!

Why has so much pain been part of my life...

Q I don't understand why has so much pain been part of my life over last 12 months?

A You are not supposed to go through each existence and suffer from beginning to end. That is not the meaning of you living an existence. You are not present to continually feel pain, to hope that at the end of that pain there will be some magnanimous understanding that will make everything all right.

There is though this...sometimes people take action and do not take action at the same time. You are at a space in which the pain has built up to a level that even you are finding it difficult to bear. The unfortunate thing is that if you continue to stay along this same stuck path, the pain will still be there to greet you. And there is another path as well. There is an opportunity for you to release this space for it is not who you are. You will not gain bigger shoulders from experiencing more than you already have. You know this do you not?

There is a time for you to experience your compassion so that the compassion of others can be allowed into your life, for that has not been an expression that you have seen the light of day of for some time. You must know and begin now to accept that a compassionate Being that a wonderful creation of the universe lives within you, it is your truest expression and it is wishing to be expressed, it does not wish to continue to experience life as you have. You have had much pain in other lives, you will see those expressions but what you will see...and this is the piece that you will take from this weekend...is that you will see that you have lived other existences in which joy, in which love, in which you were a complete expression and it is now time for you to be that space again.

So much can fall away, so much can disappear in the blink of an eye. Time you feel that it is such a ravage, you feel that time takes its toll, but you may indeed be surprised that as you feel and reconnect to that true space of you again that the components of this life that have taken so long and a toll upon you can disappear so quickly and there is no one who will know that, no one who can experience that but you.

You have gone through much suffering and it is a space now in which you do not need to do that anymore. There is a voice within you that is the very heartbeat that keeps you going that knows that there is some light at the end of the tunnel but that tunnel keeps getting longer, does it not? There is light but it is so tiny! That is because you consider yourself to be a slow train, the train that never quite reaches the end. That is not who you are.

There have been great reasons why you have manifested an expression like this and may we say to you right now there are much better reasons for you to let it go, to connect to that space of you. For you know that when you become this space, when you recognise that it is within you already and you allow that light to shine that you will affect so many people in so many ways. There is the possibility of a great shift within you and there is the expression that you wish to feel its presence now, that you are determined to not wait until you reach the light at the end of the tunnel you will just make the damn tunnel shorter. (I've been trying to do that) Yes you have, but how can you do that from the current expression of Self, how can you do that from the space of the Constricted Self?

So you are at the space, the point the cross road that you have been at before. There is the space...do you often start at the end of a book (I do skip ahead sometimes!) We are glad you do, we would like you to skip towards the end for this is your time to begin to recognise and accept your space again. You see you can allow the turn in the road to miss you again. We don't get that feeling from you and there is still the space that can allow it to pass. You have so much time, you can do it all again next time, and the time after that if you wish but it gets rather monotonous let us say...we will have to shift channels...but we hear the voice that is you and that voice wishes to be heard.

You will feel that space within you this weekend, you will feel that voice and you will take the path that will allow you to be the creator, rather than allowing everyone else to do that for you. You can restore your Energy, your health, your Being, your sense of Self...it is all possible, it is only not possible from a constricted sense of Self. So are you happy to jump to the last two pages? The rest of the story was rather boring. The end, young one does not necessarily mean the end, it can be the end of the way you have been experiencing life...would that be beneficial? (Yes)

You see all of your expressions the energies, the pains that you feel, that you have felt, all have meaning, all have reasons for being present they are all part of the universe, its Energetic frequencies and they do not wish to hang around with you any more, so stop cradling them like a loved one. Have faith in who you are, Young One, begin to trust you again...there has been a long time since you have. Know the space within you is magnificent it is not ill, it is a true compassionate Being that radiates such a brilliance, it the space that you wish and need to feel again. Know that that is your true expression and that your current form is not who you truly are.

Are there such things as negative Energies...

Q Are there such things as negative Energies or blockages in a place or is that just a belief that we hold?

A For so long the Energy of the universe has been used and misconstrued and changed and shaped in so many ways in order to keep the people in a particular box, to keep them at heel, to keep them disconnected from who they truly know themselves to be so we say to you then when you are blocked that there are dark Energies that are wishing to consume you. And so what will manifest?

If you are the same as everything else, if you are the expression of the universe there are all manner of Energies that are present but the very expression of who you know yourself to be can bring such Energies into place. So if you think that you are a Being in which darkness descends upon your every step then hallelujah sister there it is! (laughter) But that is not you, that is not the true expression of who you are. Energy is not malevolent, Energy is not here to sap and draw your very life force from your Being. Can it happen? Yes. Look at the being that is experiencing it and you will have your answer. Can the Being release it as quickly as they accepted it? Yes.

There are doctrines that have kept you separate for so long, they are expressions of Energies that have wished to manipulate you. Know that you are not that space, you do not need to accept any such expression at all! When you are the expression - and it exists within you now – when you are this expression of All That Is why would All That Is wish to send something to destroy you? Something so perfect, for that is what you are. Sometimes we are amazed at the expressions that are present on this planet, sometimes we are amazed at the way Energies treat one another and what we are continually amazed at is the resilience of your expression to say there must be more, there must be something more to my existence that keeps me going from day to day. Yes there is, it is that knowing who you truly are. In that space there is no pain, there is no darkness. When Beings of this world feel and know that to be, imagine what your planet will be then, imagine the Energy that will be sent out from this space to the rest of space and the effect that that will have on the entirety of space. And it all begins with you, this one perfect expression of Energy.

We are here because you called, we are here because you wished to be this joy and we wish you to be this joy too for we have other things we would like to do like sitting on our deck chairs sipping pina coladas watching the stars go by!

Do food and alcohol hinder us on our path...

Q Do food and alcohol actually hinder us on our path or is it how we think of them that has the impact?

A You see this is all the path of separation, it is the space of thinking where food is the object, I am separate to it. If you are connecting to your Being, if you are feeling that space of sameness then the food that you eat will be reflected in that space you will not be eating something that you feel is detrimental to you connecting to the space of All That Is. The Energy that you are will guide you towards what it is that you need and it will not matter what that food is because the Energy that is contained within the food is the same as you, the compassion that exists within each molecule will not resist against a Being who knows it to be the same. Can you see?

So the more you feel in connection with everything that you do, the more you feel that everything that you do be in connection with you. You will feel the flow, you will feel the Energy being drawn towards you, you will feel your Energy being drawn towards whatever it is that you wish to manifest. That when your space is so open that there will be no space for a fear to be present in whatever it is that you are doing or eating or experiencing because they are not present. Do you understand? (Yes, I think so) Hmmm...think so...maybe there in lies the problem! Who do you know yourself to be? (I'm still looking for that) As is everyone.

That is the purpose of you being in this existence, it is you knowing your connection and with each breath with each step displaying that frequency to all around you and then your head will be free of all its questions, a wonderful space will it not be?

Let us then...it is almost like we gave you that question so that we could segue into morning tea! (laughter) So Young One, as you move towards that table yourself, know your expression when you reach for the food, that will answer much of your question. So farewell we will be back very soon to expand your space from where it is now.

Are you always watching us?

Q As you are universal consciousness, are you observing us at all times, even when we're being intimate with someone?

A You are a curious one to ask such a question....do we watch you when you are being intimate. Yes, that is the only time. The rest of your life is of no interest to us! (laughter from the group and from DZAR)

We are curious that when you have an Energy that is present, that that is a question that you would ask, we thank you! Just keep your eyes open when next it happens for you! (more laughter!)

Practices of Becoming

In this section you'll find the Practices DZAR gives you to do at different points of the book.

You can also download the Meditation that accompanies this book from our website www.thepathofdzar.com/book1 as well as other free Meditations, podcasts and videos.

The Practice of the Expanded Being

It is time for you to feel the Energy of your Expanded Being. It is time for you to recognise this aspect which is within you, which *is* you so that you can choose to live in stronger connection with it.

Sit quietly and become aware of your current expression of Self, feel any doubts or fears that are present, feel how your body feels and notice how expansive or constricted you feel.

Make any notes you wish.

Now take four long, deep breaths and connect to your Pearl by becoming aware of that space just between your eyebrows. Feel the energy of All That Is begin to flow into the Pearl and fill your entire body.

Now notice how your body feels, notice what emotions are present, feel what this sense of Self is like, notice how expansive you feel now.

This is your Expanded Being. Some of you will feel it strongly, and for others it may feel faint at first but all will notice the difference between these two expressions of Self.

Can you feel a different level of awareness become available to you when you are connected to your Expanded Being? Do you notice a deeper feeling of calm, of compassion, of joy? Do you feel more connected to the world around you and to All That Is when you are connected to this space?

Remember, Young Ones, this is a practice and the more you do it, the more you *be* this space, the stronger your connection to your Expanded Being will become and the more clearly you will hear the messages from your Soul.

Expanded & Constricted Eyes Practice

It is time for you to feel the difference between the two expressions of Self, between your Expanded Being and your Constricted Self. It is time for you to recognise which one you are and which space you wish to make your decisions and live your existence from.

Sit quietly and feel your current expression of Self. Notice any judgements you have about yourself, others or your existence. Notice any feelings of limitation, doubt or separation you feel. This is your experience of your Constricted Self.

Now from this space, look through these Constricted Eyes at your existence. Take a moment to look at a challenge in your life or a problem you wish to solve, and as you look at it through Constricted Eyes become aware of how you feel about the situation and yourself. Notice what possibilities you see available to you.

When you are ready, take four long, deep breaths and connect to your Expanded Being using the Practice we have shared with you already.

Silently say to yourself: I am my Expanded Being; I am connected to everything and everyone; The Source Energy of creation exists within me now.

As you feel your connection to your Expanded Being expand, look again at your existence and at the challenge you chose just a moment ago.

Notice how you feel looking at your world through Expanded Eyes, notice how your world feels, notice how the situation feels, notice what possibilities you are aware of now.

As you feel the difference between these two expressions of Self, take a moment to reflect on which one you prefer. Is there one that you feel would be a better guide for you when making decisions in your life? Is there one that feels more compassionate and connected to All That Is?

And we think we know the answer to those questions, Young Ones!

Take time each day for this Practice, for you will see that the more you look at yourself and your world through Expanded Eyes, the more you will begin to change the world you live within, the more guidance you will receive from your Soul and the more joy you will experience in your life.

Practice of Understanding the Family Frequency

Sit quietly and connect to your Expanded Being.

When you can feel your connection to your Expanded Being, become aware of your family in this existence and feel the presence of your parents, your siblings and any others you consider in this group...

With the awareness of your Expanded Being, understand why you chose this family frequency in this existence...become aware of how they have contributed to your expansion, to you becoming more connected to your essence in this existence...become aware of the role you may have played in their expansion as well...

Now feel the compassionate Energy of your Expanded Being bathe your family in its glow...feel compassion for yourself in this existence and in the experiences of your family...

Feel the knowing that you are not your family...feel the knowing that any experiences of pain or limitation you have experienced within your family are *not* you...they have been signposts on your journey of expansion.

Take a moment now to feel the difference in your understanding of your family and your experiences as you view your life from the compassionate connection of the Expanded Being.

Become aware that you are beginning to see your family, your experiences and yourself in a different light because *you* are becoming more expansive and connected to your essence. Your awareness and acceptance are changing because *you* are deciding to move forward with the compassion and Energy of All That Is within you...and so it will be.

Terms Used by DZAR

by Gary O'Brien

Cloaks .... the energy of experiences that have been taken on as who we think we are. We accumulate these Energies over lifetimes and they shield our light from shining and block our connection to our Expanded Being and to All That Is.

Constricted Self ... is for many who you currently know yourself to be in this lifetime. It is the self that is expressed through the Cloaks, that feels separate from your Soul and All That Is.

Expanded Being, Essence, Soul .... all terms DZAR uses interchangeably to refer to that part of us that is eternal.

Expression of Self ... as Beings of energy, our thoughts, feelings and behaviours combine to create our sense of Self, who we know ourselves to be. They emit a frequency, an Energy that can be felt by others and felt by all things. The more you become aware of who you truly are the more you can feel the frequency emitted by all things.

Pearl ... is the connection point for your Being to connect to All That Is – it is located where your eyebrows come down to meet the point at the bridge of your nose. When it is activated, you may feel a sense of fullness or tingling and it may also feel like a rotating or spinning ball.

Separation ... is the space where you have been separated form your Expanded Being, your own source Energy, by the cloaks of experiences unlearned. It is the space where you do not recognize yourself as an Expanded Being nor that you are connected to everything and everyone.

Source, All That Is ... the energy that creates and is the Universe.

The Space of Becoming ... is the space of you knowing that you are growing and expanding along your path as your Expanded Being. It is the acceptance of time as a part of your journey and of being compassionate with yourself in the process. It is giving yourself the space to grow and realizing that you are moving step by step towards who you truly are.

Young Ones ... DZAR refers to us all affectionately as Young Ones because even though we may have had many existences, compared to All That Is we are still young on our path of becoming our Expanded Beings.

CPSIA information can be obtained at www.ICGtesting.com

262973BV00001B/8/P